THE STATE OF THE ART

JANUA LINGUARUM

STUDIA MEMORIAE
NICOLAI VAN WIJK DEDICATA

edenda curat

C. H. VAN SCHOONEVELD

INDIANA UNIVERSITY

SERIES MINOR

NR. 73

1970
MOUTON
THE HAGUE · PARIS

THE STATE OF THE ART

by

CHARLES F. HOCKETT

CORNELL UNIVERSITY AND THE RAND CORP.

Second Printing

1970

MOUTON

THE HAGUE · PARIS

First Printing: 1968

LIBRARY OF CONGRESS CATALOG CARD NUMBER 68-13341

Printed in The Netherlands by Mouton & Co., Printers, The Hague.

PREFACE[1]

This is a critical review of current American linguistic theory, directed principally—indeed, almost but not quite exclusively—towards the views of Noam Chomsky. I think those views are largely in error; but they are too powerful merely to be shrugged aside. It is necessary to meet Chomsky on his own ground. When we do this, we discover that, even if he is wrong, his particular pattern of error tells us some things about language that were formerly unknown or obscure.

Two topics that might be expected to loom large in a discussion of this sort in fact will not. Little will be said about syntactic transformations, and nothing about Chomskyan-Hallean 'phonology'. The former are helping us to discover subtle facts about various languages, and are surely here to stay.[2] The latter is, in my opinion, completely bankrupt, but is under adequate debate elsewhere.[3]

[1]The preparation of this essay was supported by a grant from the Wenner-Gren Foundation for Anthropological Research, made in 1965 and renewed in the Spring of 1966. I am deeply indebted. Because of the forceful and perhaps unpopular position I take here, I must be unusually emphatic in absolving the Foundation of any responsibility for the views expressed.

[2]For example, Lees (1960), or—especially pleasing to me—Lakoff (1965). The facts being uncovered by research of this sort are reminiscent of some of those turned up by the genius of Whorf, such as his discovery of the common feature of meaning of those English verbs that allow the formation of another verb by the prefixation of *un-*: *wind : unwind, fasten : unfasten*, and so on (Whorf c1936). In the bulk of the transformationalist literature (see Dingwall 1965) the positive factual content is sparse, but it is there, and valuable. Like the smile on the Cheshire cat, the rest can disappear, with no loss. This verbosity in technicalese is an old story in our field.

[3]The distinctive feature approach was developed by Trubetzkoy, Jakobson

The historical background presented in §1 may be of some interest in its own right, but that is not why it is included. It is included because I do not believe either Chomsky's views or my own can be fully understood except in their historical setting.

November 1966   CHARLES F. HOCKETT

---

and others of the Prague school; see *TCLP* (1929-39) passim and Vachek 1964. Joos (1948 fns. 6, 8) criticized it in the light of the initial evidence from sound spectrography. Jakobson, Fant, and Halle (1952) was ostensibly based on spectrography; see reviews by Chao (1954) and Garvin (1953). Jakobson and Halle (1956) incorporated no change, despite the cogent criticisms from various quarters; it received what seems to me to be a definitive review by Joos (1957a). Meanwhile, a strange new slant towards phonology began to take shape, represented by Chomsky, Halle, and Lukoff (1956); a later metamorphosis of this (Halle 1962), and Chomsky's sections on phonology in some of his articles, elicited Householder's loud protest (1965). Any difference between Householder's views and my own are subliminal compared to our joint disapproval of the assumptions, the techniques, and the manner of Chomskyan 'phonology'; the Chomsky and Halle reply (1965) to Householder adds nothing, but Householder's brief rejoinder (1966) does. For other criticism, see Hockett (1965 fn. 39) and the first parts of Lamb (1966).

CONTENTS

"In every science it is demanded that the investigator understand the *method* of science. He must see the reasons for its existence, be aware of its limitations, and be able to follow it, through all difficulties and seemingly endless amassments of material, consistently to a conclusion, good or bad. In all sciences there are many who can do this; it requires, at this day, no gift of genius. In the sciences that deal with man, however, there is a second demand, much harder to fulfil, to wit, that the scholar divest himself (for the time being, at least) of all the prejudices and preconceptions of his person, of his social group, or even of all mankind. So rare is this ability that it has grown commonplace to say that our social sciences are merely systematized expositions of tribal belief."

LEONARD BLOOMFIELD (1922b)

1. THE BACKGROUND

Very roughly, the first half of the twentieth century saw the following major theoretical developments in our field of inquiry: (1) the
confluence, with all appropriate turbulence, of the two relatively
independent nineteenth-century traditions, the historical-compara-
tive and the philosophical-descriptive, the practical descriptivism
of missionaries and anthropologists coming in as an important
tributary. (2) Serious efforts by Saussure, Sapir, and especially
Bloomfield, not only to integrate the positive findings of these
traditions into a single discipline but, even more, to establish that
discipline as a respectable branch of science with the proper degree
of autonomy from other branches.[4] (3) The discovery and development of the phonemic principle. (4) Attempts, particularly during
the last decade of the half-century, to put the rest of descriptive
analysis ('grammar' other than phonology) on as exact and reliable
a footing as we thought had been achieved for phonemics.

By 1950, west of the Atlantic, we had reached what seemed to be
a reasonable working consensus on these matters. Most of our
arguments were about technical details. Certain issues, however,
had been not so much settled as swept under the rug. Three of
these require our attention: (1) What is the relation between the
way a language works at a given time (in a single community) and
the way it changes through time? (2) What is the design of grammar, defined narrowly as that part of a language that lies 'beyond'

[4]The proper degree of autonomy for a branch of science is that which
enables its practitioners to forge ahead without having to wait for some major
breakthrough in some adjacent branch—though any such breakthrough, when
it does come, may require readjustments.

its phonology? (3) What is the relation of grammar to meaning? These are not ultimately separable, but we can profitably begin with the first.

1.1. Synchronic and Diachronic. Early on, we find the proponents of an integrated science of language fighting on two fronts: on the one hand, they are trying to persuade philosophical-descriptivists that one cannot afford to be cavalierly fanciful about linguistic change; on the other, they are striving to convince historical philologists that it does not make sense to confine study purely to change. Thus Bloomfield (1911) criticizes Sheffield in the following way:

The phenomena we designate as phonetic change are minutely gradual, unconscious changes of habit in the execution of certain extremely practised and therefore very much mechanized movements, namely those of articulation. Psychologically viewed, these gradual changes of habit fall into an entirely different plane — one many degrees lower as to consciousness, — from any desire or need of expressing one's thought. Such a desire or need may influence my selection of words or whole expressions, their position, their emphasis and melody, and may even impel an analogic change, but it cannot influence that remote part of my psyche that is without command or knowledge leading me, as the decades go by, to hand on to posterity certain habits of tongue-position differing by a millimetre or a few sigmas from those which my elders taught me.

Ten years later he is at the other front in his largely supportive review of Sapir's *Language*, which had just appeared (Bloomfield 1922a):

We are coming to believe that restriction to historical work is unreasonable and, in the long run, methodologically impossible. One is glad to see, therefore, that Dr. Sapir deals with synchronic matters (to use de Saussure's terminology) before he deals with diachronic, and gives to the former as much space as to the latter.

The antidescriptivist bias of philologists persisted for a long time. An apologetic or explanatory remark is frequently included in a paper that is otherwise devoted wholly to synchronic matters; for example, Swadesh (1935) says:

In determining the phonemic system of a language, only phonetic data are relevant. Historical phonology is not relevant. To base one's

spelling of a word on the form of the word in an unknown or recon-
structed parent language neither benefits historical study of language nor
provides a dependable method of accurate phonemic analysis. Historical
etymology in a matter of phonemics is an acceptable aid only when one
is dealing with an inadequately recorded noncontemporary language.
Of course, phonemes are a historical product and a step in a historical
development, but to argue from phonetic law to descriptive fact is
discovering the arguments from the conclusion when the procedure
should always be the opposite.

But merely to insist that synchronic and diachronic studies are
both valid, or even that, ultimately, diachronic studies must be
based on the results of synchronic work, is not to supply any clear
answer to our first question. During the period with which we are
concerned (up to about 1950), Saussure's mature reflections had
their impact solely through the posthumously edited *Cours* (now
we have also Godel, 1957). Wells (1947) summarizes as follows,
with references to relevant passages:

... diachronic linguistics ... differs from the synchronic branch in taking
change into account. But an immediate elucidation is needed. On the
one hand, synchronic linguistics abstracts from time and change not by
treating facts of different times as though they were simultaneous —
doing so has been a common mistake (137b-8, 202a), sometimes deliberate
(251a, 252b); but by considering a langue during a span of time too
short to show any appreciable change (142b). In short, synchronic
linguistics describes language-*states* (117a). And on the other hand,
diachronic linguistics does not directly capture the process of change.
De Saussure seems to have adopted the physicists' conception that
change may be described as a succession of states (117a only apparently
contradicts this); diachronic linguistics, taking as its data synchronic
descriptions of different states of cognate languages, infers the changes
that led from the earlier states to the later ones (128a, 140d).

Bloomfield knew, liked, and was profoundly influenced by the
first edition of the *Cours*, and took the occasion of the appearance
of the second edition to publish a brief review (1923). The next to
the last paragraph sets forth Saussure's views succinctly, as Bloomfield understood them, and endorses them as his own:

This rigid system, the subject-matter of "descriptive linguistics," as
we should say, is *la langue*, the language. But *le langage*, human speech,

includes something more, for the individuals who make up the community do not succeed in following the system with perfect uniformity. Actual speech-utterance, *la parole*, varies not only as to matters not fixed by the system (e.g., the exact phonetic character of each sound), but also as to the system itself: different speakers at times will violate almost any feature of the system. This brings us to "historical linguistics," *linguistique diachronique;* when such personal and temporary features of *la parole* become general and habitual in the community, they constitute a change in the system of *la langue*, — a sound-change or an analogic change, such as are recorded in our historical grammars.

Note particularly, in the first sentence above, the epithet *rigid*; and note that the rigid system is interpersonal or superpersonal; that is, individual differences within a speech community are external to the system. A few years later, reviewing Jespersen's *Philosophy of Grammar*, Bloomfield expresses the same view even more clearly and forcefully (1927a; I have added italics for emphasis in the second of the paragraphs cited):

> For Jespersen language is a mode of expression; its forms express the thoughts and feelings of speakers, and communicate them to hearers, and this process goes on as an immediate part of human life and is, to a great extent, subject to the requirements and vicissitudes of human life. For me, as for de Saussure ... and, in a sense, for Sapir ..., all this, de Saussure's *la parole*, lies beyond the power of our science. We cannot predict whether a certain person will speak at a given moment, or what he will say, or in what words or other linguistic forms he will say it. Our science can deal only with those features of language, de Saussure's *la langue*, which are common to all the speakers of a community, — the phonemes, grammatical categories, lexicon, and so on. These are abstractions, for they are only (recurrent) partial features of speech-utterances. The infant is trained to these features so thoroughly that after earliest childhood the variabilities of the human individual and the vicissitudes of human life no longer effect them. They form a rigid system, — so rigid that without any adequate physiologic information and with psychology in a state of chaos, we are nevertheless able to subject it to scientific treatment. A grammatical or lexical statement is at bottom an abstraction.
>
> It may be urged that change in language is due ultimately to the deviations of individuals from the rigid system. But it appears that even here individual variations are ineffective; *whole groups of speakers must, for some reason unknown to us, coincide in a deviation, if it is to result in a*

linguistic change. Change in language does not reflect individual variability, but seems to be a massive, uniform, and gradual alteration, at every moment of which the system is just as rigid as at every other moment.

After another five years, Bloomfield's terminology has changed slightly but his views are essentially unaltered. The first chapter on historical linguistics in his *Language* (1933) begins with this well-known bridge passage:

The language of any speech-community appears to an observer as a complicated signalling-system, of the kind that has occupied us in the preceding chapters of this book. A language presents itself to us, a any one moment, as a stable structure of lexical and grammatical habits.
This, however, is an illusion. Every language is undergoing, at all times, a slow but unceasing process of *linguistic change*. [Written records attest to this: the English of King Alfred's day is now unintelligible.] ...
The speed of linguistic change cannot be stated in absolute terms. A speaker has no difficulty, in youth, in conversing with his grandparents, or, in age, in conversing with his grandchildren, yet a thousand years — say, thirty to forty generations — have sufficed to change the English language to the extent that we have just indicated. During these generations, it must have seemed to each London-English mother that her children were learning to speak the same kind of English as she had learned in her infancy. Linguistic change is far more rapid than biological change, but probably slower than the changes in other human institutions.

The earlier 'rigid' is now 'stable', but it seems unlikely that either term was meant in any special technical sense.

The problem of the compatibility of rigidity and change appears in another context: that of sound change. Sapir and Bloomfield were both neogrammarians, in the sense that both accepted the principle of the 'regularity of sound change' as an empirical fact and as a necessary working assumption: when Sapir needed a convincing example of sound historical linguistic method for an article he was preparing (1931), he chose as paradigmatic a striking episode in Bloomfield's work on Central Algonquian. There was a difference of opinion, at least at one stage, as to the exact nature of the mechanisms responsible for the empirical fact. In his review of Sapir's *Language*, from which we have already quoted, Bloomfield takes Sapir to task on one point:

It is important, in the expansion of our science to its just province, that we should not commit the obvious fault of losing the historical accuracy of our predecessors; accordingly one regrets an error of principle in the historical part (190), where the author speaks as if the contrast of vowels in *foot : boot* were a matter of sound-change now in progress. Of course, sound-change while in progress does not show itself to us in this or any other way; the contrast in question is due to a sound-change dated about 1700, followed by varying distribution of the resultant forms in Standard English ... .

For Bloomfield's view, compare the quotation given earlier from his review of Sheffield, and the discussion in his *Language* (1933); in essence this view is also mine.[5] I do not know whether Sapir revised his opinion on this matter, but if he did his student Swadesh apparently inherited the earlier theory, expressed as follows at another point in his 1935 'Phonemic Principle':

... Phonetic change [i.e., sound change] must consist in the change of the norm of a sound or of one of its positional variants. Change in a phonemic norm does not affect the actual phonemic pattern unless the phoneme thereby comes to coincide with some other phoneme or splits up into more than one phoneme. *The intermediate step in coalescence of phonemes is the condition of phonemic interchange. ...*

(The emphasis is mine.) We learn elsewhere in Swadesh's paper that 'phonemic interchange' refers to the situation in which a word, or each word of some set, alternates freely between two different phonemic shapes: e.g., for some speakers of English, *soot, room, hoop*, and some others all with either [ú] or [úw]. This is just Sapir's earlier view. Hill's fine paper of the same period (1936), on the other hand, is closer to Bloomfield's position. Both views are alive today, and it may be that both are in fact compatible with the findings of the neogrammarians, though personally I do not believe so. For the present discussion, the point is that the Sapir-Swadesh theory is an overt effort to render rigidity and change

[5]But not the latter part of Bloomfield's chapter (1933 pp. 365ff.); see below in the present essay, and Hockett (1965 §6; 1966, §4). The theory of sound change had to remain largely phenomenological until spectrography revealed to us how wildly variable are the actual sounds of speech. Only then could it be reformulated as I have in the sources referred to.

compatible, by finding the seeds of change in certain features of a language that are not, after all, so rigid. Bloomfield found this 'solution' unacceptable, but presented none of his own; instead, he admitted honest ignorance ('whole groups of speakers must, for some reason *unknown to us*, coincide in a deviation, if it is to result in a linguistic change').

That Bloomfield in 1933 still clung to the notion of *la langue* as a *social* norm from which every individual may deviate without necessarily changing the norm, is attested in §20.11 of his book (pp. 365ff), where he reports what he believes to be distinctions quite regularly maintained in the speech of certain Middle Westerners that are nevertheless nonphonemic in 'the language'. Wittingly or unwittingly, Saussure had packed two intersecting contrasts into his single pair of terms: some of the time *langue* means 'habit' while *parole* means 'behavior', but at other times *langue* means 'social norm' while *parole* means 'individual custom'. But just what is meant by 'the community', whose norm is the *langue* in the second of these senses? How large is it? A family? a village? a nation? A moment's thought should be enough to show that this view—the view that rejects the distinction just described—is incompatible with the known facts of dialect variation, and hence ultimately incompatible with what we know of linguistic change.

The Saussurean way of relating the synchronic and the diachronic, essentially unmodified by Bloomfield, is echoed in various other articles. In 1942, in a paper that, like Swadesh's of 1935, was really purely descriptive, I made some effort to pull apart the two dimensions that Saussure had failed to distinguish, but in every other way what I said was purely Saussurean. In this paper I speak in terms of possible preliminary orderings of one's data: if one pays attention to its spatial or social distribution, the resulting analysis after the ordering is synchronically comparative (we would now say 'contrastive'); if one pays attention to temporal distribution, the resulting analysis is historical. Then there is this passage:

But historical and [contrastive] ... study implies first the completion of *descriptive* analysis of each of the temporally or spatially or socially grouped ranges of material. Descriptive procedure establishes the fiction that the various utterances to be dealt with have no temporal or spatial or social order. This fiction is valid only when the time or space or social span covered by the material is relatively small; it breaks down, for instance, when we take our records of Old English as a single unordered set. If the actual course of change in speech behavior [the wrong term; read: habits] through time be pictured as a curve then the approximation of descriptive technique to the actual situation can be represented by a tangent to the curve at a given point.

Of course, this adds a rhetorical figure that Saussure might not have used. We find the same figure, expressed much more elegantly, in a passage published in 1965; this is fifteen years after the end of the fifty-year span with which we are primarily concerned, but is worth quoting: even here, from the master Chao, there is nothing new as over against the Saussurean view:

The idea of a purely synchronic stage of a language is methodologically comparable to the idea of velocity or of acceleration at a given instant. The instantaneous value is defined as the limit of average values over a length of time, including the instant, as the length vanishes. In a sense, then, it is a scientific fiction set up for methodological convenience.

Note, especially, in the later of these quotations, not only the resort to metaphor, but also the prevalence of terms like 'illusion', 'convenience', 'fiction'.[6] What is fascinating is that these terms appear not in apologetic acknowledgment of defects in an approach, but actually as *justification*! This is the background of Harris's 'game-playing' linguistics of the late 1940's and early 1950's,[7] and of the controversy between 'God's-truth' and 'hocus-pocus' in the 1950's.[8] Look again at what Bloomfield asserts in 1933: 'This [rigidity], however, is an illusion'. But *whose* illusion? The linguist's?

[6]The last of these terms is, of course, especially prominent in Twaddell (1935).
[7]Harris's long series of papers and reviews begins with (1942 (1941 is only a precursor, though significant) and ends in (or is followed by a long silence after) 1957; most of them appeared in *Lg* and *IJAL*. His book (1951), which in part summarizes the earlier work, must have been completed several years earlier, for I read it in typescript in 1948 or 1949. The atmosphere of game-playing is unmistakable; see the end of §1.3 below, for further discussion.
[8]The terms, I believe, were Householder's. The main forum for this discussion was *IJAL*, about 1950-1955.

If so, then he should disillusion himself and try to come to grips with reality, or else stop pretending to be a scientist. The speaker's? If so, then the illusion of the speakers of a language is a crucial part of the reality with which the linguist must deal—one man's subjectivity is another man's objectivity—and part of the linguist's task is surely to try to understand how such illusions come about and are maintained.

But these questions were not asked at the time, and the basic question—how a language can be at every moment 'rigid' and yet be constantly changing—was not answered. In the years around 1940 it was not our mood to want to deal with this question. We wanted to brush it aside and get on with the task of describing languages and of developing better techniques for such description. The battle to render descriptivism respectable had been won. It had become safe to politely ignore the protests of a few disgruntled but feeble oldsters; indeed, some of the oldsters were actively on our side, and we left it to them to argue with their unreconstructed age-mates. Beginning early in the 1940's we find a long series of purely descriptive papers that do not even bother to specify that they are purely descriptive; Wundt and Delbrück would both have been mystified. One of the first is Harris's 'Morpheme alternants in linguistic analysis' of 1942; this, and a representative sample of those that followed, are reprinted in Joos's *Readings in Linguistics* (1957b), but anyone concerned with tracing developments in this period must take the Joos collection only as a very sketchy outline. Let me merely list, in alphabetical order, the names of some of these post-Bloomfieldian descriptivists: Bloch, Haas, Harris, Hockett, McQuown, Nida, Pike, Swadesh, Trager, Voegelin, Wells. Most of this group had had at least some exposure to traditional historical linguistics during their own training; but, with the change of emphasis, by the later 1940's we were admitting some newcomers to our ranks with no historical training at all.

Meanwhile, in Europe, Saussure's influence had been different. I shall speak almost exclusively of the Prague school, since this is another major route by which Saussure's teachings were eventually spread to the United States; this implies no derogation of the contributions of other scholars, such as Jones or Palmer. Saussure was himself a skilled historical linguist, one of the original group of neogrammarians; his growing realization of the validity and importance of purely synchronic. study in no way impaired his judgment of our hard-won knowledge of the facts of linguistic change. The Prague school phonologists welcomed Saussure's incisive endorsement of descriptivism, but rejected his neogrammarian views on linguistic change as 'atomistic', which perhaps they were, and thus as incompatible with the systematic patterned nature of a language at any one moment; they cured the toothache by executing the patient.[9] This orientation was brought across the Atlantic especially by Jakobson, who arrived in the early War years. There was then an increasingly profitable interstimulation of Praguian and American descriptivism, especially in phonology; but, at the same time, here was one more factor contributing to a bad break in the tradition of historical linguistics in this country.

At this point we leave the first issue—rather up in the air, because that is where it was at the half-century. Since I have spoken of a break in the tradition, I must reassure the reader that I am well aware of the continued intelligent devotion to historical linguistics of such scholars as Emeneau, Hall, Haugen, Hill, Hoenigswald, Lehmann, Twaddell—to name a few who surely deserve the epithet 'post-Bloomfieldian'—as well as of many fine scholars whose training had been, for better or worse, somewhat freer of Bloomfield's influence. A tradition can split, and then be broken along one branch while it continues along the other (like a used wishbone). My main concern here is, by definition, with the branch where the break occurred.

[9]See passim in *TCLP*, and Vachek (1964). As has often been pointed out, for example by Bloomfield (1933, pp. 354ff.), the scholar who overtly rejects the neogrammarian hypothesis may not thereby be precluded from doing excellent historical work. The discussion of these matters has always been very confused, and different people rejecting (or accepting) the hypothesis are not always reacting to the same thing. Jakobson's deprecatory remarks about the neegrammarians in his theoretical discussions are, in my opinion, unimportant when measured against such a masterly accomplishment as his outline of the history of Russian phonology (1929).

1.2. The Delimitation and Design of 'Grammar'. In this section the term 'grammar' is in general to be understood in the old and honorable sense that excludes phonology. Whether or not grammar in this sense includes lexicon is one of the points at issue. The relation of grammar to meaning is another. On these points I will try to be no more ambiguous than are the sources we quote.

Our second and third issues, it will be remembered, have to do with the design of a language other than its phonology, and with the relation of grammar to meaning.

In 1914 Bloomfield expressed the classical view as to the whole design of a language in the following way:

The first task of the linguistic investigator is the analysis of a language into distinctive sounds, their variations, and the like. When he has completed this, he turns to the analysis of the semantic structure, — to what we call the morphology and syntax of the language, its grammatical system.

Here we have the very opposite of a proposal that grammar and semantics are separable. A language has forms (words, morphemes, sentences); forms have meanings; the correspondences between forms and meanings *are* the 'semantic structure', which *is* the 'grammatical system'. This view of Bloomfield's never really changed. In the late 1920's he says (1927b):

De Saussure's system is ...: (1) actual object, (2) concept, (3) acoustic image, (4) speech utterance; the series to be reversed for a hearer ... . The totality of this is *le langage;* and the segment formed by the two purely mental terms (2) and (3) is *la langue*, the socially uniform language pattern. De Saussure's careful statement lays clear the point at issue: What he calls "mental" is exactly what he and all other linguists call "social"; there is no need for the popular finalistic terms. We shall do better to drop (2) and (3) and speak instead of a socially determined correspondence between certain features of (1) and (4).

With or without the 'mental' apparatus that Bloomfield proposes be set aside as terminologically redundant (for that is a different issue, not the one to which we are at the moment addressing ourselves), we have the same picture as before: two sets of things, forms and their meanings, and the systematic ties or correspondences between them.

In 1943, still speaking of this same pair of things, Bloomfield adds:

To earlier students, language appeared to have a third aspect, inter-mediate between form and meaning; this aspect was usually called *function*. Thus, a word like *apple* not only meant a certain kind of fruit, but also functioned as a noun, serving as the subject of verbs, as the object of prepositions and transitive verbs, and so on. Careful study, however, shows that features like these are a part of the form; they are the formal features which come into being when two or more forms are combined in a larger form. Thus, the word *apple* enters into phrases with preceding adjectives and, except for certain very special expressions, is always so preceded (*an apple, the apple*); ... and so on. A form's privilege of occurring in any one position is *a function* of that form, and all its various functions together make up its *function*. In sum, the func-tion of a speech form consists merely of formal features which appear when it serves as part of a more inclusive form.

Now, to understand this we must know not only what Bloomfield meant by 'meaning', but also what he meant by 'form'. Shapes, in terms of phonemes and their arrangement, are only part of what he meant by 'formal features'. This points to one of the most obscure aspects of Bloomfield's views, perhaps best represented by the first part of the chapter 'Form-Classes and Lexicon' in his 1933 book. He makes a fundamental dichotomy of the materials of a language into *lexicon* and *grammar*. Lexicon is forms; gram-mar is the patterns of arrangement of smaller forms in larger ones. Within lexicon we find 'minimum meaningless elements'—phonemes —certain combinations of which are 'minimum meaningful elements'—morphemes. Within grammar, in a parallel way, we find 'minimum meaningless features of arrangement'—Bloomfield's *taxemes*—certain combinations of which are 'minimum meaningful features of arrangement'—his *tagmemes*. To render this even more complicated, it turns out that by 'arrangement' Bloomfield does not mean merely the geometrical location of elements relative to one another, but several rather diverse things: taxemes (or tagmemes) of *order*, which we have just described, are one type, but there are also features of *selection*, of *modulation*, and of *phonetic modification*. Observe, in particular, the lowly position assigned by this view to phonemics—hidden in a corner, as it were, at the lowest size-level of 'lexicon'.

As far as I know, the only post-Bloomfieldian who has tried to develop this particular frame of reference is Pike.[10] To many of us in the 1940's it did not make sense; it still does not to me, though I can now explain my dissatisfaction with it much more clearly than I could have twenty years ago. Let us consider merely order ('arrangement' in the narrow sense). One cannot have a purely abstract arrangement, without any things *in* the arrangement. And one cannot say that two arrangements are same or different unless the same elements occur in both. Consider elements x, y, z, and w, about which we assume merely that when we encounter one of them we can tell which one it is. Obviously we can say that xy and yx are instances of different arrangements. But what can we say about xy and zw? Are they instances of the same arrangement or of two different arrangements? We cannot say. Of course, if we are also informed that x and w are A's, while y and z are B's, then we can assert that xy and zw are instances of different arrangements, since the former is AB and the latter is BA. But how are we (as analysts) or the speakers of a language informed about A and B? An assertion such as 'x is an A' is based on distributional information, which brings the matter back to the geometrical arrangements of actual forms, not of *types* of forms denoted by symbols like our 'A' and 'B'.

The proposed distinction between taxeme and tagmeme (at least, between taxeme and tagmeme of 'order') seems unworkable. To be sure, in some cases the relative position of two elements is a mechanical matter about which the speaker can do nothing: we say /béyks/, with the inflectional affix after the stem, and cannot achieve some other meaning by saying */sbéyk/ with the same elements in the other order; and in other cases it is functional: *matchbook* versus *bookmatch*. But it is hard to see how a 'minimum meaningful feature of arrangement' can be viewed as a 'combination' of 'minimum meaningless features of arrangement' in any way that is remotely parallel to the way in which a Bloomfieldian morpheme can be interpreted as a combination of phonemes. Bloomfield's taxemes and tagmemes were an attempt to formalize what many of his contemporaries, including Sapir, were calling 'grammatical processes'; but the formalization was based on an analogy that will not work.

As to meaning, Bloomfield's views have been widely misunderstood. The commonest misinterpretation is probably based on a few scattered passages such as the following (which, indeed, appears prominently in the first paragraph of the chapter on Meaning in his 1933 book—p. 139):

We have defined the *meaning* of a linguistic form as the situation in which the speaker utters it and the response which it calls forth in the hearer.

This sounds as though he were saying that the meaning of a specific act of speech, as a historic event, is the behavioral antecedents and consequences of that act of speech. I am quite certain that this was not his view. Bloomfield despised pomposity of statement; but his laudable drive towards simplicity of expression occasionally led him to an ambiguous wording. The meanings of speech forms are the things and situations, or kinds of things and situations, encountered by the speakers of the language. Speech forms have habitual associative ties with meanings as thus defined. The meaning of a form is not, to be sure, in the 'mind' of the speaker or hearer (not as Bloomfield understood and used, or refused to use, the term 'mind'); but the associative ties between meanings and forms are, indeed, mediated by the central nervous systems of speakers and hearers, by neurological mechanisms that are largely unknown to us but with which, as linguists, we need not be concerned. By virtue of these associative ties, a particular act of speech in a specific behavioral setting is able to link behavioral antecedents and consequences together in certain ways. That this was his view is attested by the ways he handled materials in specific languages and by the general tenor of his theoretical discussions, marred only occasionally by a lapse such as that quoted above; perhaps the clearest statement is in the first two pages of his late article 'Meaning' (1943).

A different source of difficulty, particularly confusing, as we shall see, to his followers in the 1940's, is represented by the following passage, again from page 139 of his 1933 book:

The situations which prompt people to utter speech, include every object and happening in their universe. In order to give a scientifically accurate definition of meaning for every form of a language, we should have to have a scientifically accurate knowledge of everything in the speakers' world. The actual extent of human knowledge is very small, compared to this.

Anthropologists and anthropologically oriented linguists disturbed by this particular view have proposed that he was simply wrong: that in order to discuss the meanings of the forms of some language one merely needs to know the rest of the culture of its speakers, rather than everything about the physical and biological world in which they live.[11] But, in principle, just what would one have to investigate in order to describe 'completely' the lifeways of a human community? Two approaches are essential. One is that of the 'outside view': investigation into the details of the physico-geographical environment, the changing spatial distribution of the population, its genetic types, and so on. The other is the 'inside view': the total set of behavioral patterns, of expectations, of habits of interpretation of things and events, of the members of the community. For example, if ax handles are customarily manufactured from the wood of a certain tree, then the botanical identification of that tree species is an outside view matter, while the typical ways of obtaining the wood, of fashioning the handles, of using them, of discarding them when they wear out, and of talking about all these activities, are inside view.[12] The task of analyzing and describing a language is the business of the linguist. But since a language is part of a community's totality of lifeways, the linguist's

[11]Hoijer will, I hope, forgive me if my memory is faulty: I think I remember remarks to this effect from him, but cannot find them in his publications.
[12]This is explored in Hockett (1964). Quite independently, there has arisen a group of young American anthropologists who are actively developing much the same approach: Goodenough, Lounsbury, Frake, Sturtevant, Conklin, Romney, and several others. For this see some of the essays in Romney and Andrade (1964), and all those in Hammel (1965).

task is a proper part of the total task of the ethnographer, who in principle seeks to analyze and describe *all* the lifeways of a community. The difficulty which Bloomfield saw in dealing with the meanings of speech forms can indeed be to some extent bypassed by describing meanings in terms of the rest of the community's lifeways. But the difficulty then reappears in ethnography as a whole, just in that ethnographic description depends for 'completeness' on the accuracy and completeness of outside-view information, and the outside view is nothing other than Bloomfield's 'scientifically accurate knowledge of everything in the speakers' world'. Bloomfield's only error, then, lay in ascribing just to language a source of difficulty that in fact pertains to all of culture.

We post-Bloomfieldian descriptivists of the 1940's were dissatisfied with several aspects of Bloomfield's portrayal of language. We believed that our own views were derived at bottom from his, that we were clarifying confusing details in his view by applying procedures and ways of thinking that he had taught us. But our views actually differed from his in two important respects.

(1) In the first place, as we have just seen, Bloomfield had repeatedly insisted that the discussion of meaning is beset with difficulties; from this he himself inferred, not that scientific linguistics is impossible, but merely that our characterization of a language should always start from form rather than from meaning. The approach via meaning held too much danger of introducing irrelevant philosophical apriorisms, or of imposing on one language semantic categories actually relevant only for some other. During the 1940's some of us suspected that it might be possible to determine the forms of a language, and all the patterns by which they combine into larger forms, without any reference to meaning at all. Some decided that this was not only possible, but, indeed, the only rigorous procedure, even if occasional resort to meaning might be a useful practical shortcut.[13] A few even went so far as to interpret Bloomfield's recommendations as implying that any resort to meaning was 'mentalistic' and thus taboo—something that he

[13]The 'shortcut' view was particularly that of Harris (especially 1951); see also Hockett (1952a).

never said or implied, and a procedure that he never followed in his own work and that he would have rejected as impossible.[14]

We also considerably shifted the meaning of the term 'grammar'. We came to think of 'grammar' largely as the patterns by which meaningful forms (not mere phonemes) combine or arrange into larger forms—an *autonomous* set of patterns, unrelated to meaning, or at least susceptible to analysis and description as though it had nothing to do with meaning. This was not to deny that utterances actually spoken often carry meaning (or convey information, or have partly predictable consequences, or something of the sort); but it was a separation of grammar, or of grammar-and-lexicon, from semantics. Perhaps a complete description of a language would have to deal with semantics too, but this should be done separately, not mixed in with the description of the grammar.

(2) In the second place, a few of us, particularly Trager, Bloch, and I, came early to disagree sharply with Bloomfield's notions about the relation of phonemics (or phonology) to the rest of language.

We have seen above how, at least during one period, Bloomfield set up the dichotomy between lexicon and grammar ('form' and 'arrangement') as basic. Yet even more fundamental than this, in his view, was the dichotomy between morphology and syntax, with the *word* as boundary. This fundamental notion cuts through everything else. It was so basic a tenet in his thinking that in many of his writings it remains tacit. The problem in phonemic analysis was, as Bloomfield saw it, first and foremost to be certain of the

[14]The clearest statement of this most extreme view was formulated by Hoenigswald (1949) as spokesman for a fairly large group of temporarily dizzy investigators: 'In language, certain noises (speech sounds) combine into certain arrangements to the exclusion of certain others; strongly aspirated sounds like those initial in English *pin* or *kin* occur before stressed vowels except when certain consonants precede ...; the sequence of sounds spelled *-en* follows the sequence *ox-* but not the sequence *fox-* ...; *to* is found after *want* but not after *must; barking* is found before *dog, meowing* before *cat, ill-gotten* before *gains* and so on. It is the task of linguistics to make such statements exhaustive and economical, either for a given speech community at one place and time ... or in terms of historical change.' Just such cleancut statements as this began to show us the absurdity of the viewpoint.

The misinterpretation of Bloomfield's views on meaning is discussed beautifully in Fries (1954).

articulatory-acoustic features that serve to keep *words* apart. The fate of words in phrases—whether word boundary is audible or not, whether or not certain words lose their inherent stresses, and the ways in which speech melody is superimposed—all this was also important, but constituted a separate portion of phonology. One might almost say that Bloomfield split phonology into morphological phonology (phonemics) and syntactical phonology, though he used no such pair of terms. You will find this opinion expressed or reflected in his writings as early as 1916 and as late as the 1940's. As far as the published evidence shows, Sapir agreed. This was almost identical with the Prague phonological doctrine. I remember viva voce arguments with Jakobson in the early 1940's in which we were unable to come to any agreement, probably because neither of us was able to grasp the approach of the other. (See also Haugen 1949.)

Trager, Bloch, and I, on the contrary, took the dichotomy between phonology and grammar-and-lexicon to be more fundamental than that between morphology and syntax. We considered it the business of phonemic analysis to determine and tabulate all those articulatory-acoustic features that serve to keep the *utterances* (not merely the 'words') of a language apart. This system of features would, of course, include any relevant differences of speech melody, contrasts of stress, and whatever phonetic stigmata might turn out, when we had examined the grammatical structure of sentences, to signal boundaries between words (if, indeed, such boundaries were signalled at all) But we regarded words as grammatical units, not as phonological or overriding ones, and thus considered the morphology-syntax dichotomy to be a subdivision within grammar, not necessarily paralleled by any comparable break-up of the phonological system.

It was preeminently Pike who stuck to the Bloomfieldian view during the 1940's (and later), thus prolonging the theoretical argument.[15] I am inclined to say that, today, the phonological views

[15]Pike (1947); Bloch (1948); Hockett (1949); Fries and Pike (1949); Bloch (1950); Pike (1952); then the argument frayed out, no one having convinced anyone else.

of the transformationalists are the rather direct descendants of those of Bloomfield, Sapir, and the Prague school, while what they call 'taxonomic phonemics', insofar as it is not purely a straw man, derives ·from the Bloch-Trager-Hockett notions of the 1940's.

As we developed this modified approach in the 1940's, our watchword was *rigor*—though we had no very rigorous definition of it. Precision of statement was far more important to us than whether anyone could understand us; amazingly, we thought we had learned this from Bloomfield! Trager published a presumably rigorous account of French verb inflection that is, indeed, almost impossible to read (1944). Bloomfield reacted with about as much violence as he ever allowed himself to show towards a colleague in print; his reproof (1945) began with one of the wisest passages he ever penned:

, Traditional grammars base their description on orthography, they sometimes employ clumsy procedures, and often they resort to repetition instead of assembling forms which present a common feature. This last habit is pedagogically useful, when one does not carry it to the length of causing difficulty by sheer bulk, so as to swamp the noteworthy feature.

Systematic description, on the other hand, tries to assemble all forms that have any common feature and to unite them under a single statement. Now, the basic uniformity in language is the mere recurrence of forms and constructions. The partial resemblances between forms which we describe in morphology are often so whimsically irregular that a rigorous statement has practical disadvantages. It may take more discourse to describe a few eccentric forms than it would merely to cite them. The author of a rigorous description finds difficulty in making it watertight; even Panini left some holes. The reader finds difficulty in interpreting, applying, and combining the separate statements; this, too, would be true of Panini's grammar even if one could mend the superficial faults (such as unwritten ditto marks). A less rigorous statement may be more useful even for scientific purposes.

These remarks were introductory to an alternative presentation of the facts of French verb inflection. The treatment is really not very good—not nearly so good as some of Bloomfield's earlier technical accounts of similarly intricate sets of facts. But as a demonstration of the point he was trying to make it would have failed no matter how elegant, because we were in no mood to listen. My own reaction at the time was perhaps not completely typical, but it was also not completely idiosyncratic: I felt that Bloomfield was betraying his own cause.

We sought 'rigor' at all costs. In searching for a 'rigorous' approach to grammar (as we had newly defined it, to include lexicon but exclude phonology), we found a guide in the assumptions and procedures that had proved so fruitful in phonology. This was reinforced by an incipient parallelism in the technical terms we were using:

(1) Just as phonemes are (or were then generally assumed to be) the minimal elements in phonology, so morphemes were to be the minimal elements in grammar. Just as phonemes appear, in some instances, in the guise of two or more allophones, so morphemes may vary in shape; hence something analogous to the procedures that enable us to group allophones into phonemes ought to serve to group morpheme alternants into morphemes. This was Harris's proposal in 1942. It was I, under the influence of certain European developments that were coming to my attention,[16] who clinched the parallelism by proposing (1947b) the term *allomorph*.

(2) In phonemic structure or patterning, sometimes called 'phonotactics', one is no longer interested in anything merely allophonic. First by implication, later explicitly, it was recognized that phonemic arrangements are a matter of clumping of phonemes into small groups (initial consonantisms, syllable nuclei, etcetera), which in turn cluster into larger groups, and so on—hierarchical patterning in phonology.[17] This reinforced a tendency in grammatical thinking that Bloomfield's writings did little to combat (though he was inconsistent): in grammar, too, we were not to be

[16]Again my memory is faulty. In the spring of 1946 I read an article in someone else's copy of a European journal, which set me to thinking about duality of patterning. For a long time now I had thought that the article was Martinet's 'La double articulation linguistique'; but a check shows that that article was not published until 1949. I think what I read in 1946 must have been by Martinet, conveying proposals that we have since learned to ascribe also to Hjelmslev, and perhaps ultimately to Saussure.

[17]This is hinted at by Bloomfield (1933: 'compound primary phonemes' and the like); it is more or less implicit in all discussions of phonotactics; but the first overt statement known to me is Pike and Pike 1947.

interested in the actual shapes of morphemes, be they stable or alternating, but only in the ways morphemes cluster together into ever larger forms, and this way is obviously hierarchical.

Slowly and painfully, largely under the leadership of Harris, we constructed a view of the design of grammar based on our view of the design of a phonological system, freeing our procedures and terminology of any vestiges of the 'grammatical process' (or 'taxeme') kind of thinking, until we had achieved what we seemed to have been seeking: a pure *item-and-arrangement* model of grammar.

This particular term, true enough, appeared in print only in 1954; but the article I published in that year had been written four years earlier. It is interesting to note that we no sooner achieved a pure item-and-arrangement model (not yet called that) than we began to wonder whether it was really what we wanted. Harris challenged it even as it was a-building; Bolinger challenged it more or less from the sidelines (1948); of course Pike challenged it; and I did. My 1954 paper has on several recent occasions been misinterpreted as a defense of item-and-arrangement and an attack on item-and-process.[18] The paper must have been badly written, since my actual intention at the time was nothing of the kind. I wanted to examine the then prevalent way of thinking and to suggest that the item-and-process model, and perhaps even other models, also deserved serious consideration. Be that as it may, it is not quite correct to characterize our predominant theoretical leanings in the 1940's as 'phrase-structure grammar' (Postal 1964a), since that term occupies an exact position in a frame of reference much more highly formalized than any we were using. But it is true that the only obvious formalization (within that particular frame of reference) of the item-and-arrangement

---

[18]Once by Halle (1962, fn. 9), once by Teeter (1964, p. 203). Their mis-interpretation is not entirely their fault; several of my students have said that, until I told them otherwise, they thought the 1954 paper was intended as a defense of item-and-arrangement. Late in 1964 I explained orally to Teeter what had been my actual intention in the 1954 paper and in the particular clause he had quoted from it. He insisted that his interpretation was right anyway.

model is phrase-structure grammar; transformations require item-and-process.[19]

1.3. The Half-Century. The foregoing leaves out many details and variants: it slights Pike's progress towards tagmemics, Trager's proliferation of powers of three,[20] and my own fumbling steps towards stratificational theory. But most of the details of these came later. It also says too little of the persistent doubters (such as Bolinger), whose role should not be underestimated merely because our reaction to them was delayed by our preoccupation with other problems or approaches—indeed, we would have done better to have heeded them earlier.

By 1950 we had quite recovered from certain queer views that had once been prevalent. For instance, I have just recently been reminded (by Hahn's warm and charming reminiscences of Edgerton, 1965) of a dispute of the late 1930's that I had completely forgotten. The issue was put in the form of a question: 'Can one analyze a language one does not know?' Older scholars such as Edgerton, Hahn, Kent, or Sturtevant, who had spent years mastering languages to which many predecessors had devoted their lives, tended to say 'no'; on the other hand, Boas and Sapir sent their graduate students for a year (or even a summer or so) of 'field work' with a hitherto undescribed language and allowed them to write up their data as a doctoral dissertation. It is rumored that when Newman returned to New York from his field work with the Yokuts, Boas asked him slyly, with no outward sign of humor, 'Well, did you get the whole language?' Of course, the issue was not expressed clearly; but I, for one, was quite taken in, and assumed when I went to the Potawatomi that I did not have to strive for any measurable degree of practical control of the language in order to analyze and describe it. The facts could be stored in notebooks and file boxes as they were gathered; they did not also have to be stored in my head. It is not surprising that my account of the

---

[19]This seems to have been recognized by Chomsky (1957, various footnotes). At least, Chomsky does not reach Postal's absurd conclusion that item-and-process and item-and-arrangement are 'the same thing' (Postal 1964a).

[20]An early formulation in Hall and Trager (1953); a late one in Trager (1963).

language (1948, but written 1939) was so inadequate. Linguists of the Summer Institute group were saved from this because they all knew that they had to learn their languages thoroughly in order to accomplish their missions. For the rest of us, the War closed the argument out, as it gave us assignments in which there was simply no choice between learning and analyzing—we had to do both.

On the other hand, a new crop of strange opinions had sprung up. One of the most puzzling of these was the completely arrogant notion that nobody had ever done any syntax. The historical germ of this one may have been the fact that very little had been published on the syntax of American Indian languages, with which so many of us had served our apprenticeships. But in the face of vast quantities of excellent data on Latin, Greek, and Sanskrit, to say nothing of Bloomfield's Tagalog (1917) and other isolated shorter treatments, I guess we must really have meant that nobody had ever done any syntax *right*. I do not remember clearly just what we thought doing it right would involve, except for the common notion that to do it right one would have to abjure all reference to meaning. Of course, these opinions were not shared by everyone. But they were in the air, and some of us breathed pretty deeply.

Relative to the three issues set forth at the beginning of §1, the state of affairs at the half-century can be described as follows:

(1) In our synchronic work, we accepted without question the Saussurean-Bloomfieldian characterization of a language as a 'rigid' system, and sought to match its rigidity with our rigor. We ignored the whole problem of the implications for language design of the fact of linguistic change, and vice versa.

(2) Our model for grammar, as for phonology, was item-and-arrangement, much more narrowly and precisely than Bloomfield's or Sapir's had ever been, though some of us were developing some doubts about too mechanical and complete a parallel between grammar and phonology.

(3) There were disagreements about the validity of using meaning for grammatical analysis, but a consensus that grammar and semantics were separable and should be separated. The traditional (and Bloomfieldian) direct correlation of meanings on the one hand, formal features on the other, was incorrect; between semantics and phonology stood

grammar-and-lexicon, as a separate and autonomous subsystem of the whole language.

It is now my opinion that on all three points the consensus was wrong, and that any theory of language design that accepts any one of the three is faulty.[20a]

I believe that Trager, Bloch, and I were essentially correct in the early 1940's, as over against Bloomfield then, Pike then or now, or Chomsky and Halle now, in our view of the status of phonology within language design. We were wrong, of course, in accepting without challenge the Saussurean-Bloomfieldian notion of 'letter-sized' phonemes as the ultimate building-blocks in phonology; but I, at least, had begun to relinquish that view by the end of the war (1947a, 1947c). I also believe there is convincing evidence for 'hierarchical structure' in phonotactics—for which, as far as I can see, neither the Chomsky-Halle scheme nor algebraic grammar makes any provision.

Hockett-Lamb stratificational theory (Hockett 1961, Lamb 1964a, 1964b, Gleason 1964) is approximately correct in its place-ment and handling of phonology, though also giving no overt recognition to hierarchical structure, but is otherwise almost entirely misguided. Consider Bloomfield's pair 'meaning' and 'form', taking the latter to mean nothing but phonological shape. Stratificational theory handles the enormously complex corres-pondences between meaning and form by decomposing these cor-respondences into a succession of mappings between successive 'strata'—at least two, at most (so far) five (Lamb, viva voce; now see Lamb 1966). This is all fine provided we regard the machinery of strata, of elements on each stratum, and of mappings from stra-tum to stratum as descriptive conveniences. In any one case, they are then either helpful or not, and we can use them when they are, pull some other tool out of our kit when they are not. But stratifi-cational theory proposes that all this machinery is not only in our

[20a][Added just before release of the present essay:] I have just been reminded that Wallace Chafe's thinking in the last few years (as shown in several published articles and in an unpublished manuscript of which I have a copy) seems closely to parallel mine in rejecting these three firm notions of the 1940's.

description but also in the language and even, in some sense, *in the speaker*. For this there is no shred of evidence, nor do I understand how there could be. And the theory reinforces our tendency of the 1940's to assume that the organization of affairs on other strata is more or less parallel to organization on the phonological stratum. I believe this is quite impossible.

Pike has given us some remarkably important insights: phonological hierarchical structure is one; his brief exposition of linguistic-like approaches to the discussion of other phases of culture (1954, the first few sections) is another. These contributions are all the more striking because they are couched in a terminology and style as confused, inconsistent, and redundant as I have ever encountered in any field of scholarly endeavor (see the last paragraphs of Hoijer 1955 and McQuown 1957; the hope expressed in the latter has so far been vain). Tagmemics chokes on its own terminological complexity. Science always makes things as simple as possible. Tagmemics, like a cult, makes them as obscure as possible. Detailed exegesis would be a losing battle; the garden is so overgrown with weeds that the only sensible procedure is to plow it all under and plant afresh.

Only one other current dispensation in linguistic theory is prominent enough to deserve mention here, but that is the most prominent of all: Chomsky's theories. Syntactic transformations, in either the Harris or the Chomsky version, reject number (2) of the three points listed earlier, to yield a special sort of item-and-process model of grammatical design that is not only more powerful but also, in my opinion, much more realistic than any -item-and-arrangement model can be. We shall here note some of its sources of power; the matter of realism is deferred to §6.1. Recall Bloomfield's remarks of 1945: 'Systematic description ... tries to assemble all forms that have any common feature and to unite them under a single statement.' Transformations are a great help in this, in that limitations of cooccurrence can be stated once for a whole group of transformationally related phrase-types, instead of separately for each (Harris 1957, Chomsky 1957). Again from Bloomfield: 'The reader [of an overly 'rigorous' description] finds difficulty in interpreting, applying, and combining the separate statements.' The effective ordering of rules does much to combat this difficulty. Transformations are heuristically valuable: if nothing else told us so, transformational tests would quickly reveal that the predicates of *I found the village* and *I walked a mile* are not parallel (Chomsky 1957). Outside of syntax, ordered rules are a wonderfully clarifying device in morphophonemics.

To be sure, transformational treatments of specific data are still usually too cumbersome and hard to follow, but we may hope that that will pass. It is not uncommon for an innovation to be much more complicated than really necessary when it first appears—look at the earliest television sets!

But we must remember that transformations are largely a corrective to certain temporary extremisms of the 1940's, a reintroduction, with improvements and under a new name, of certain useful features of the Bloomfieldian and Sapirian view of language, that we had set aside. Harris, much more than the rest of us, was playing a carefully calculated methodological game in the years just before transformations made their appearance: he was asking 'How much of relevance can we discover and say about a language if we constrain ourselves to such-and-such limited, but explicitly formulated, tools and approaches?' Repeatedly the clear answer was 'Not nearly enough'; whereupon more tools and approaches were added— finally, those that we call transformations.

We must also remember that transformations are not a theory, but only a possible ingredient of a theory. On this score, particularly since Harris was Chomsky's mentor in linguistics, it will be worth our while to note something of Harris's style of exposition and the attitudes it seems to reflect. His oral discourse used to be peppered with remarks more or less like this: 'Of course, this is only one way to do it; but let us see where it gets us.' Similar asides occur, though more sparsely, in his writings. This manner was pleasant for his colleagues, since it signalled a laudable scholarly modesty and left plenty of room for the rest of us with our various differing opinions and interests. But it also signalled something else. At bottom, the source of Harris's modesty and tolerance seems to have been a particular philosophical orientation: the Real Truth (at least about language) is not attainable, so we might as well have a good time sharing our occasional dim glimpses in its direction, and not worry too much about Ultimates. Harris's central concern has always been, not with data, but with techniques for handling it; thus—in common with some of the rest of us at the time—he was quite prepared to doctor his data if such doctored raw-material was better than the real facts of a language for some methodological demonstration.

It is fair to say, I believe, that Harris has been a superb *methodologist*, but never at any time a *theorist* of language. A theoretical concern with language must try to deal not only with techniques of analysis, but also with what language is to its users, and with how it performs its role in human life. Harris had rarely had anything to say on such issues (Voegelin and Harris 1947 is an exception). Very early in his career he wrote (1941): 'The Prague Circle terminology ... gives the impression that there are two objects of possible investigation, the Sprechakt (speech) and the Sprachgebilde (language structure), whereas the latter is merely the scientific arrangement of the former' (cf. Hockett 1952b). The first part of this is impeccable; see below (§5.4). The part beginning with 'whereas', if taken literally, would reduce linguistics to an unmotivated and unprincipled pastime; for one thing, the phrase 'scientific arrangement' has no clear meaning. Yet Harris's attitude seems never to have changed. Accordingly, his paper on transformations (1957) was presented with no discussion of wider implications, merely in the spirit of methodology—as though to say, here is one more interesting way in which the linguist can arrange his data.

While I have no desire to underestimate either Chomsky's originality or the importance of what he may have learned from other predecessors, I believe we can discern in his student-mentor relation to Harris the source of some of his views. No one as intelligent as Chomsky could fail to be stimulated by Harris's methodological inventiveness; no one as serious-minded as Chomsky could long rest content with Harris's theoretical nihilism. Unlike his teacher, and more like some of the rest of us, Chomsky must theorize. Chomsky's direct references to Harris in his publications are always marked by the most delicate respect and politeness. Yet it is Chomsky who has been most insistent on the distinction between theory and heuristics (1957 and repeatedly since). The point is surely correct, but not new to most of us; the strength with which it is made is understandable only as an overreaction to Harris's orientation. Now, as a point of departure for theorizing about language, Harrisian descriptive linguistics, with its almost sole emphasis on data-manipulation, is terribly narrow. It ignores much of the tradition of our field. It affords no clue as to the possible functional relation between empirical investigation on the one hand, generalizing and theorizing on the other. Indeed, Harris's consistent refusal to draw any broader or deeper inferences from his analytical investigations leads naturally, if not.inevitably, to Chomsky's opinion that heuristics has little or nothing to contribute to linguistic theory.

Lacking any explicit guidance as to where to turn for a broadened basis for linguistic theory, Chomsky was forced on his own resources and taste, and turned towards the abstract fields of logic, mathematics, and philosophy, rather than to science. If Harris's work suggested either of these directions, it was the former. Indeed, a number of us at the time, in our search for 'rigor', were gazing longingly towards mathematics (cf., for example, Hockett 1952a, 1952c). In any case, the move was reasonable, since linguistics (or language) surely has interconnections of various sorts with these scholarly endeavors just as it has with anthropology, psychology, and biology. Drawing selectively from these fields, and adding from his own ingenuity, Chomsky has been constructing an elaborate and coherent theory of language which differs strikingly from any proposed by linguists or philologists, or by psychologists or philosophers, during the last hundred years or more. This is important. By moving away from the rest of us at a wide angle, Chomsky has achieved a different perspective. We cannot reject his opinions merely because we fail to see, from our angle of view, what he thinks he can discern from his.

Chomsky's theory, like transformations as a technique, rejects the second of the three errors of the 1940's listed earlier. But it has so far uncritically incorporated the first and the third. I believe that these are fatal flaws. The exposition of the theoretical orientation to which I am objecting, and of my reasons for the objections, will occupy the next sections of this essay.

2. THE CHOMSKYAN ORIENTATION

The following nineteen numbered points are an attempt at a concise summary formulation of Chomsky's current views (i.e., as of late 1965). The wording is my own, though I have freely used scraps of transformational jargon without quotation marks; all direct quotations are from Chomsky (1965), and the page numbers are given.

For the sake of accuracy I sent two successive versions of this list to Chomsky, who very kindly supplied criticisms and comments. Even the present version is not entirely to his liking, but his residual disagreements or addenda are transmitted to the reader directly after the four points involved (C2, C12, C16, C17). It must be remembered that this partial 'endorsement' of my formulation is in no way binding on Chomsky. In the first place, agreement on wording does not necessarily imply agreement on what the wording means. In the second place, every investigator reserves the right to change his views.

C1. The vast majority of the sentences encountered throughout life by any user (= speaker-hearer) of a language are encountered only once: that is, most actually used sentences are novel. This is a central fact for which any linguistic theory must provide.

C2. Any user of a language has access, in principle, to an infinite set of sentences. In practice, all but a finite subset of these require too much production time to be usable in any possible circumstances; but these practical limitations are extraneous to the language.

[Chomsky: 'It might be worth mentioning that production time is not the only factor that makes sentences unusable. Internal

THE CHOMSKYAN ORIENTATION

complexity (in some poorly understood sense) would be another
factor, as would obviousness, obvious falsehood, meaninglessness,
etc.']

C3.   The user knows the grammar of his language (or: knows
his language), though not in a sense of 'know' that would imply
that he can explicitly tell others of his knowledge. The task of
characterizing a language can thus be described as that of specifying
just exactly what one must know to know the language. This
body of knowledge constitutes the user's *competence*. The user's
competence *is* the grammar of his language. (Note that by 'the
user's competence' we mean his own personal version, not the
language of his speech community in some generalizing or common-
denominator sense. Also, what we mean here by the grammar *of* a
language is not to be confused with any investigator's explicitly
proposed grammar *for* a language.)

C4.   A user's *performance*—what he actually says and hears—
reflects his competence, but is also conditioned by many other
factors. A theory of performance is not the same as a theory of
competence. The central concern of linguistics is the latter.
Moreover, any search for a correct theory of performance depends
for its success on the degree of success we achieve in the search
for a correct theory of competence.

C5.   A convenient device for barring from consideration lin-
guistically irrelevant factors in performance is to imagine 'an ideal
speaker-listener, in a perfectly homogenous speech-community,
who knows its language perfectly and is unaffected by such grammatically irrelevant conditions as memory limitations, distractions,
shifts of attention and interest, and errors (random or characteristic) in applying his knowledge of the language in actual performance' (p. 3).

C6.   Since the user's competence is a *mental* reality, linguistics is
necessarily mentalistic. (This rejects naive behaviorism, but implies
no opposition to materialism.)

C7.   Probabilistic considerations pertain to performance, not to
competence as we have defined it above. Surely the user of a
language has a certain knowledge of probabilities, but this know-

ledge constitutes a mental reality distinct from the grammar of the language. Knowledge of probabilities, along with various other factors, influences actual performance, but there is no reason to suppose that it has anything to do with the organization of grammar.

C8. The distinction between grammatical and nongrammatical sentences (whether absolute or a matter of degree) applies to competence, not to performance. The degree of *acceptability* of an actually performed utterance is a different matter.

C9. Meaningfulness, like grammaticality, pertains to competence. But these two are distinct—there are grammatically well-formed sentences that are meaningless, and nongrammatical sentences that are meaningful at least in the sense that, when performed in an appropriate setting, they convey the information they are intended to convey.

C10. The grammar of a language is a finite system that characterizes an infinite set of (well-formed) sentences. More specifically, the grammar of a language is a *well-defined system* by definition not more powerful than a universal Turing machine (and, in fact, surely a great deal weaker).

C11. At present there is no known algorithm for computing or 'discovering' the grammar of a language: 'no adequate formalizable techniques are known for obtaining reliable information concerning the facts of linguistic structure' (p. 19); 'knowledge of grammatical structure cannot arise by application of step-by-step inductive operations (segmentation, classification, substitution procedures, filling of slots in frames, association, etc.) of any sort that have yet been developed within linguistics, psychology, or philosophy' (p. 57).

C12. Yet almost every infant performs successfully the task of language acquisition. It must be, therefore, that the infant brings to this task at least the following: an *innate* system for the production of an indefinitely large set of grammars of 'possible' human languages; and the *innate* ability to select, from this set, the (or: a) correct grammar for the language of his community, on the basis of a small sample of dimly perceived and imperfectly performed actual utterances in their actual settings.

[Chomsky: 'I agree with what is said, but would like to add that
the infant's innate system must include much more, e.g., an
algorithm for determining the structural description of an arbitrary
sentence given an arbitrary grammar.']

  C13. An explicit formulation of the innate grammar-producing
system just mentioned would constitute a *general grammar* (or
general linguistic theory). If we had such, then the characterization
of any specific language would require only that we plug in appropriate values for certain of the variables (or arbitrary constants) in
the general grammar.

  C14. The innate grammar-producing system is a well-defined
system in the sense of C10, just as is the grammar of any single
language.

  C15. It is at least plausible that the grammar of a language
consists of three components: (a) The *syntactic* component 'specifies
an infinite set of abstract formal objects, each of which incorporates
all information relevant to a single interpretation of a particular
sentence'; to do this, each 'abstract formal object' must be not
merely a string of formatives but that plus a specific *structural
description*. (b) The *phonological* component 'determines the
phonetic form of a sentence generated by the syntactic rules'.
(c) The *semantic* component (which possibly is the same for all
languages) 'determines the semantic interpretation of the sentence'
(all p. 16).

  C16. In searching for the grammar *of* a language, one may
propose various explicitly formulated grammars (or partial grammars) *for* the language. The search is appropriately constrained by
C10, and usefully guided by C15. A grammar proposed *for* a
language is *descriptively adequate* 'to the extent that it correctly
describes the intrinsic competence of the idealized native speaker'
(p. 24). A descriptively adequate grammar for a language is *prin-
cipled* to the extent that it conforms to a general linguistic theory
of the type mentioned in C13.

  [Chomsky's comment on the second sentence: 'I think the reference should be to C12 and C13, not C10. I think the reference to
C15 is perhaps not clear.' The significance of the reference to C10

will emerge in our subsequent discussion; I am glad to add that to
C12 and C13. The reference to C15 is merely intended to suggest
that, if we have a general notion of the organization of a grammar
(as set forth in C15), that is surely going to be heeded as we work
on any particular language.]

C17. One also searches for a correct general linguistic theory
(C13). A theory proposed in this search is descriptively adequate
'if it makes a descriptively adequate grammar available for each
natural language' (p. 24). A descriptively adequate general theory
is *explanatorily adequate* to the extent that it approximates the
innate grammar-producing system, and other innate capacities, of
the infant (C12).

[Chomsky: 'I think a useful distinction can be made between an
epistemological and a psychological variant of the question of
deeper adequacy. Perhaps we could say that a general theory
achieves "explanatory adequacy" if it provides for the selection of
grammars that are descriptively adequate (this is the epistemological
variant) and, simply, that it is true to the extent that it approximates
the inner grammar-producing system, etc. (the psychological
variant). Now in fact we have no evidence about the innate
grammar-producing mechanisms other than what we can determine by studying the linguistic problem of justifying grammars, so
that in practice, the two problems collapse. In principle, however,
they are distinct, and it is the psychological problem of truth that
is the important one. I'm sure I'm not saying this very clearly, but
I think the point is important.'[21]]

C18. The proposal in C15 has to do with the format of the
grammar of a language; that is, the structure of the ideal speaker-
listener's competence. It says nothing as to how the user *employs*
his grammar in either the production or the reception of sentences.
Nor is this an issue in the search mentioned in C16.

C19. A linguistic *change* is a shift from one grammar (of the
set of all grammars of all 'possible' human languages, C12) to

[21]This comment from Chomsky is so thoroughly off-the cuff (remember, from
a letter, not from a publication) that I have hesitated to include it here. I shall
make nothing of it in what follows.

another (presumably similar) one. It is essential to distinguish between *system-conforming* and *system-changing* events: the latter are (relatively) rare. In particular, it is important not to mistake an awkward or inaccurate performance for one that is really symptomatic of a change in underlying competence.

3. WELL-DEFINED AND ILL-DEFINED

The second sentence of C10 (§2) alludes to a branch of modern mathematical logic known as the theory of computability and unsolvability. The allusion is crucial, not incidental. As Chomsky says (1965, p. 8):

Although it was well understood [in the nineteenth century] that linguistic processes are in some sense "creative", the technical devices for expressing a system of recursive processes were simply not available until much more recently. In fact, a real understanding of how a language can (in Humboldt's words) "make infinite use of finite means" has developed only within the last thirty years, in the course of studies in the foundations of mathematics.

What Chomsky says in this passage may be right or wrong, relevant or irrelevant, but we are entitled to no opinion on the matter unless we know what he is talking about. We must undertake an exploration into intellectual territory unfamiliar to most linguists.

I shall quote from an excellent recent book on computability and unsolvability (Davis 1958). In the introduction (pp. xvi-xvii), the author gives an informal definition of an 'effectively calculable function': for instance, if we are presented with any positive integer n, obviously we can calculate the corresponding value of $n+1$. He then shows that the easy acceptance of the intuitively obvious definition of 'effectively calculable' seems to lead to some rather strange dilemmas. The first paragraph of Chapter 1 (p. 3) reads as follows:

We shall proceed to define [with formal rigor] a class of functions which we propose to identify with the *effectively calculable functions*, i.e., with those functions for which an algorithm that can be used to compute their values exists ... . Our point of departure is the remark that, if an algorithm for performing a task exists, then, at least in principle, a computing machine for accomplishing this task can be constructed. Such a computing machine is *deterministic* in the sense that, while it is in operation, its entire future is completely specified by its status at some one instant.

To this last sentence Davis appends a footnote:

This excludes from consideration both analogue computers and computers that contain "random" elements.

The type of computer developed in the theory is called a *Turing machine* (after the British mathematician A. M. Turing who devised this approach); a *universal* Turing machine (mentioned in C10) is one of a special type, essentially simple in design and yet so powerful that, if a function can be computed at all, it can be computed by a machine of this sort (pp. 64-5).

By a *deterministic* (or *well-defined*) *function* we shall mean any function subsumed by the stated frame of reference: that is, any function computable in any of the several precise senses of that term developed in the theory, but also any function that is specified with sufficient explicitness that its *noncomputability* can be *proved* within the theory. A *well-defined system* is any system (physical, conceptual, mathematical) that can be completely and exactly characterized by deterministic functions. Thus, an *ill-defined system* is one excluded from the theory of computability and unsolvability by the proviso in Davis's footnote. Of course, we must carefully ignore any prejudicial connotations of the term 'ill-defined'.

In the next sections (§§3.1-9) we consider a series of examples.

3.1. It is necessary to assume that the infinite ordered set of all positive integers, 1, 2, 3, ..., is well-defined. Mathematically, this set can be taken as the image of the number-theoretical identity function $f(n) = n$, and this function is indeed computable in Davis's formal sense, hence deterministic. But the set of all positive integers is also the *domain* of $f(n) = n$, so that the computability of the function does not help us. We must have some independent guarantee that our requirements are met.

Perhaps it is enough to observe the unlimited open-endedness of the Arabic notation for positive integers. Given any positive integer in this notation, of however many digits' length, we know exactly how to write down the next larger integer, and, in principle, could always write it down in a finite amount of time. We have to agree that it is irrelevant that, for most integers, only an Elder God would have the requisite patience. That is, we have to agree on this if we are going to be able to make any use of the theory of computability (except for essentially trivial problems about strictly finite sets), for if the positive integers are not accepted as well-defined, this theory has no place to stand—nor, indeed, does most of mathematics.

3.2. Consider, next, the set of all n-place decimal approximations to the value of π: for the first few values of n the approximations are 3.1, 3.14, 3.142, 3.1416, 3.14159. Like our first example, this is an infinite set. There is an algorithm which enables us, given any positive integer n, to compute the n-place approximation; therefore the set is well-defined. Since π is itself exactly characterized by this infinite set of approximations, we are entitled to assert that π is well-defined.

3.3. What is the set F of all positive integers n for which positive integers a, b, and c exist such that $a^n + b^n = c^n$? We know that 1 and 2 are in F, since, for example, $1^1 + 1^1 = 2^1$, and $3^2 + 4^2 = 5^2$. In the seventeenth century, Pierre de Fermat reported that he had found a proof that no integer greater than 2 is in F; but his work was lost. By the late 1950's it had been shown that no integer less than 4000 (except 1 and 2) is in F. Clearly, continued testing of successive integers would disprove Fermat's conjecture if a counter-instance were found, but could never *prove* the conjecture, since there would always remain more integers to test. The indirect approach of the theory of computability is called for. If F is computable, then a search for an algorithm is in order, though actually finding one would still be, at least in part, a matter of luck. If F is not computable, then the search is useless. To date, no one (except perhaps Fermat) has demonstrated either the computability or the noncomputability of F, but it seems almost certain that the set is well-defined: that is, that one of these two alternatives is demonstrable.

3.4. What is the set S_f of all possible scores that can be earned by an American football team in a single completed game, playing by intercollegiate rules? (These are occasionally changed, so that, to be precise, we should have to specify a year.) A safety wins 2 points, a field goal 3, a touchdown 6, and a conversion after touchdown 1 or 2. Any score, then, must be of the form $a + 2b + 3c + 6d$, where a, b, c, and d are nonnegative integers and $a \leq d$. Every nonnegative integer except 1 can be expressed in this form. But this does not mean that every nonnegative integer except 1 is a possible football score. Even against no opposition, scoring requires time, and play is confined, at most, to slightly more than 60 minutes of time in.[22] A score of 1,000,000 is obviously impossible. The highest score on record is 227.[23] Could speed and skill be increased (and strength of opposition decreased) to squeeze this up to 228? Possibly. To 229? Perhaps. The fact that we can easily name an integer greater than any member of S_f does not mean that there is a precise maximum element in S_f. The set is neither computable nor noncomputable: it is *ill-defined*.

This has some important implications for the use of mathematical methods.

There is a familiar principle in mathematics expressed as follows: if a set of integers (or of elements of certain other kinds, that will not concern us) has an upper bound, it has a least upper bound. Given a set of integers K, an upper bound b is an integer such that, if x is any integer in K, then $x \leq b$. Now let B be the set of all upper bounds of K. The principle asserts that if B contains any integers at all, it contains a particular one, say b', that is as small as any integer in B: that is, such that if b is any integer in B, then $b' \leq b$.

---

[22]If at the end of any quarter the gun goes off during a play, the play is completed. The clock does not run during an attempt at conversion.

[23]Dickinson vs. Haverford Grammar School, 1900, final score 227-0. In 1916, Georgia Tech had run up 222 to 0 against Cumberland (Tennessee) at the end of the third quarter, and the game was stopped. The rules have changed since these games. Also, customs have altered: such unevenly matched teams simply do not play an official game any more. (Menke 1963.)

But now consider our set S_f of all football scores. This is a set of integers, and we have agreed that the integer 1,000,000 is greater than any integer of S_f; that is, that 1,000,000 is an upper bound of S_f. Yet S_f has no least upper bound. For if it did have, that least upper bound would be the largest possible football score, which we have seen is meaningless. The point is, of course, that the least-upper-bound principle is applicable only to well-defined sets.[24]

Another important consequence is this. Formally, a set is *infinite* just if it can be put into one-to-one correspondence with one of its proper subsets; otherwise it is *finite*. Thus, the set of all positive integers is infinite because it can be put into one-to-one correspondence with the set of all positive even integers, and every positive even integer is a positive integer but not vice versa. On the other hand, the set of all integers from 1 to 10 inclusive, or the set of all English letters from A to Z, is finite. Now, the test for the infinitude or finiteness of a set *cannot be applied* in the absence of well-definition. In everyday terms, we would probably all agree that S_f is finite; but the everyday loose sense of 'finite' differs from the formal sense, so that such an agreement has nothing to do with the matter.

It is interesting to note that the set S_b of possible baseball scores (earned by one team in one completed game, under Major League rules) is well-defined: any nonnegative integer. If there is a tie at the end of nine innings, the rules provide for as many additional innings as necessary until the tie is broken. Of course, no actual game goes on forever; but there is nothing *in the rules* to prevent an indefinitely long game and an indefinitely high score. For that matter, there is nothing *in the rules* to prevent the piling up of an indefinitely large score during a single inning of one team.

3.5. So far our examples have been numerical. Let us consider

[24]Another case of this sort is the 'perfect mile' that sports writers like to speculate about: that is, the exact shortest time in which any human runner can run a mile. The time it takes to run a mile (subject to the imperfections of stopwatches and the like) is a real number, and real numbers have the bound property discussed in the text. But the system is not well-defined, so that the property is irrelevant, and the 'perfect mile' is a myth.

a nonnumerical case: chess. The rules of chess are quite exact. A given distribution of pieces on the board is a *state*. The rules specify, first, a fixed *initial* state. They specify, second, by means of the provisions for moves and captures, exactly what states can immediately follow any given state: that is, the permissible *state-transitions*. They specify, third, exactly what states are *terminal*, and assign all terminal states to three pairwise disjunct classes: White wins; Black wins; and Draw. A *game* (in the sense of a *playing*) of chess is a finite sequence of states of which the first is the initial state, the last is a terminal state, and each state-transition is permissible. Two games are (formally) identical if, and only if, they are identical state by state. The number of possible distinct games is enormous but finite. A computer can be programmed to run through all possible games, register the outcome of each, and print out the best move for each player for each possible state. In this sense, chess is computable, and hence well-defined. On a computer the size of the Earth, the running time is estimated at about 10^{37} years.[25]

Some points in the Chomskyan view of language can be exemplified (or, perhaps, parodied—though that is not my intention) in terms of chess, though other important aspects, such as meaning, cannot. A chess player's 'competence' in the everyday sense is how well he plays; in the Chomskyan sense, it is how well he knows the rules of the game. His 'performance' may be expert or clumsy even if he know the rules perfectly. I am not quite sure what an 'ideal' player would be: possibly only one who had memorized the results of the computation described in the preceding paragraph, but possibly just any player who never makes an illegal move. A 'grammatical' move is a state-transition that does not violate the rules; a 'nongrammatical' move would be, for example, an initial move of pawn to king's fifth. The actual occurrence of a

[25] I have to take this on faith from Frank Rosenblatt, who cited me the figure from an article by Bremerman that I have not been able to locate. The figure given in the text may be compared with the estimated age of the earth, about 10^{10} years. Calling the latter an 'earth lifetime', the estimated time for the computation is 10^{27} earth lifetimes.

strategically poor move, or even of a 'nongrammatical' one, does not change the rules. Any number of actually played games in which no pawns were taken en passant would not eliminate the rule that provides for that type of pawn capture. On the other hand, if a World Chess Congress voted to eliminate the provision for taking a pawn en passant, there would be a real change: chess as we have known it would be replaced by a more or less different game.

Physical board and pieces are not part of chess, but mere mnemonic aids; some players get along without them (one recalls the story of the famous Russian master Ivan Prokokofieskovitch, who played twenty-six games simultaneously blindfolded—and lost every single one of them). When the aids are used, it can happen that a piece is moved or removed accidentally, or by cheating, or that an illegal arrangement of pieces persists for a while. If a 'game' is 'completed' without detection and correction of the discrepancies, then the participants have in fact not played chess, though they may never know this. Performance is subject to divers vicissitudes and uncertainties, but performance is not competence.

3.6.   Let us take another look at American football. The set of all possible scores, we know, is not well-defined; but perhaps the game is well-defined in all other respects. I believe it is not. Like chess, football is characterized by explicit rules; but, whereas the physical board and peices for chess are only mnemonic aids, the field, the ball, and the team members for football are indispensable. Chess is *quantized*—like a digital computer. Football is not. Successive downs are discrete, but the action within a single down is continuous, the possible actions form a continuous array, and the possible outcomes for a single down form a continuum. Thus there is 'slippage', as in the analog computer—set aside, it will be remembered, by Davis in his footnote.

In part, this fuzziness is eliminated by resort to officials and their rulings. In one sense there is no sharp boundary between, say, those acts that count as attempted pass interception and those that count as interference with the pass receiver. But the boundary is rendered sharp by the officials: what has just happened is attempted interception if the officials say so, interference if they say so. Similarly, if, when the ball is downed, there is any uncertainty as to whether or not the offense has earned a first down, the officials bring the line out and make an either-or ruling. But this quantization is incomplete. It is quite impossible to say (and, for football and our enjoyment of it, totally unimportant that we cannot say) that at the end of a particular play the ball is *exactly* on a spot it has occupied previously in the same game or in some other. This being so, we might judge that two actually played games were very similar, in one or more of a number of respects; but the rules afford no single persuasive criterion for deciding that two actually played games are formally the *same*. Therefore there is no way of specifying—to say nothing of computing—the set of all possible 'distinct' games. We are clearly in the area of ill-definition.

Baseball is very different. The rules (and the officials) quantize everything so sharply—balls, strikes, fouls, outs, runs, hits, errors—that the game is perhaps well-defined (I am not absolutely sure). Ignoring points of audience interest, such as the demeanor of specific players, on which the rules are silent, we can probably define formal identity between actual games, and render the set of all possible distinct games enumerable (though clearly infinite).

3.7. Next we turn to a social institution: middle class American table manners, say as of the first decade or so of the present century. Despite the codification of proper manners by Emily Post, and the feedback effect of this on actual behavior, I think it would be wrong to propose that the system is in any significant sense governed by rules—the explicit codification is largely after the fact. A fortiori, the system is not well-defined. Here is what Boas had to say (1911):

... I think it is not difficult to show that certain groups of our activities, whatever the history of their earlier development may have been, develop at present in each individual and in the whole people entirely sub-consciously, and nevertheless are most potent in the formation of our opinions and actions. Simple examples of this kind are actions which we consider as proper and improper, and which may be found in great abundance in what we call good manners. Thus table manners, which on the whole are impressed vigorously upon the child while it is still young, have a very fixed form. Smacking of the lips and bringing the plate up to the mouth would not be tolerated, although no esthetic or other reason could be given for their rigid exclusion; and it is instructive to know that among a tribe like the Omaha it is considered as bad taste, when invited to eat, not to smack one's lips, because this is a sign of appreciation of the meal. I think it will readily be recognized that the simple fact that these habits are customary, while others are not, is sufficient reason for eliminating those acts that are not customary, and that the idea of propriety simply arises from the continuity and automatic repetition of these acts, which brings about the notion that manners contrary to custom are unusual, and therefore not the proper manners. It may be observed in this connection that bad manners are always accompanied by rather intense feelings of displeasure, the psychological reason for which can be found only in the fact that the actions in question are contrary to those which have become habitual. It is fairly evident that in our table manners this strong feeling of propriety is associated with the familiar modes of eating. When a new kind of food is presented, the proper manner of eating which is not known, practically any habit that is not in absolute conflict with the common habits may readily establish itself.

3.8. I assert now that *no physical system is well-defined.*

This requires some interpretation, for which one of Davis's remarks is of help. He points out that a computer of the sort required for the theory of computability is '*deterministic* in the sense that, while it is in operation, its entire future is completely specified by its status at some one instant'. We can transfer this characterization from computers to physical systems in general by saying that a physical system is 'in operation' only until it breaks down, either spontaneously or through some outside agency; and by specifying that by the 'entire future' of a physical system we mean to include not only its behavior until it breaks down but also the breaking-down itself. A physical system would be 'deterministic', and hence well-defined, only if it conformed to Davis's characterization as just interpreted. The requirements are quite stringent, but the interpretation receives support from Davis's footnote. If a physical system were not deterministic in just this sense, it is hard to see how it could be completely and exactly characterized by deterministic functions; any such characterization would be only an approximation.

In order to be deterministic in this sense, a physical system would have to have no moving parts, and would have to be isolated from the rest of the physical universe. For if there are moving parts then there must be thermodynamic indeterminacy—random wear and tear, the effects of which are predictable only in a gross statistical way. And if the system is not isolated then there must be relativistic indeterminacy: the impingement of individually unforeseeable influences from outside, whose effects, again, are only statistically predictable. But the only physical system with no moving parts is an elementary particle (if, indeed, there is any such thing), which is not isolated; and the only system that is isolated is the whole physical universe (if there is any such thing), which contains moving parts. Thus the assertion is proved.[26]

It is important not to confuse well-definition with *stability*, a property that every physical system has to one or another degree— as do, also, such ill-defined nonphysical systems as table manners. A muon, left to itself, will break down only after an average lifetime of 2.2×10^{-6} seconds, so that it is very unstable relative to everyday human affairs; but that is long enough for light to travel a respectable distance (about .660 kilometers), and is a virtual eternity relative to certain known nuclear reactions that take place in about 10^{-23} seconds. A human being remains in the states we class as 'being alive' for several decades. An electron will apparently last forever if left to itself—but no electron lives in solitude for very long, even in intergalactic space. Designers of computing machines go to great lengths to guarantee a practically usable stability span: one wants the machine to behave itself at least long enough to complete the run on a specific problem. So the machine is made tremendously massive relative to the unpredictable behavior of its smallest components (electrons are shunted around in batches of about 10^{12}), and is strongly insulated against any intrusion from outside other than a negligibly tiny or catastrophically large one. Even so, every machine has a fair measure of down time.

[26]This paragraph is virtually a direct quotation from Hockett (forthcoming-a). The so-called quantum indeterminacies do not have to be mentioned separately, since they are subsumed under the two sources of indeterminacy given.

Davis's reference to computing machines, as a point of departure for the theory of computability and unsolvability, is clearly not a reference to physical systems; he is not confusing stability with determinacy or well-definition. Note that the second sentence of the paragraph we have cited from him includes the phrase 'at least in principle'. These words play the same role in mathematical discussion of this sort that the word 'leading' plays in the advertiser's 'best of all leading brands': these hedgings supply a formal escape hatch if one is needed, but are soft-pedalled in the hope that the audience will overlook them. What Davis really means is a computing machine that would perform exactly as we tell it to: in other words, a *conceptual* computer. The hardware we might use as a 'realization' of the conceptual computer is okay as long as it is sufficiently stable, but is in fact related to the conceptual computer only as physical board and pieces are related to chess.

3.9.   As a final pair of examples we shall consider the set of all hydrocarbons of the methane series, and the set of all structural formulae for those hydrocarbons. To construct a formula of this set, take n C's, $2n + 2$ H's, and $3n + 1$ short line segments, where n is any positive integer. Arrange the C's in a row and insert a line segment after each but the last. Attach an H at each end and one H above and one H below each C. Thus, for $n = 1, 2, 3$ we get the formulae for methane, ethane, and propane:

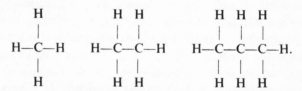

Each formula is an idealized and flattened-out model or picture of a molecule of the hydrocarbon in question. It is clear that nothing but a shortage of time and patience—and motivation!—prevents us from writing down the formula for the case of $n = 1,000,000$, or even more. 'In principle' we can make the formula as long as we want; here the hedging phrase has its customary meaning, which is to say that we agree to ignore anything that keeps the assertion from being true, by virtue of which the assertion becomes true. The set of formulae is well-defined, and infinite.

Not so the hydrocarbons themselves. As n increases, the chain twists in space more and more, and stability decreases. The probability that a methane-series hydrocarbon molecule with large n will actually form (in the rest of nature or in that special segment of nature we call a laboratory) decreases as n increases, as does the life-expectancy of such a molecule if it does form. There is no well-defined 'longest possible' methane-series hydrocarbon molecule; yet the number of chemically possible distinct hydrocarbon molecules is not infinite. This is a fact left out of account in the chemist's system of notation, just as that notation requires only two dimensions as over against the three occupied by the molecules, and just as it represents, say, a carbon atom by the completely nonpictorial symbol 'C'.

This pair of examples is instructive in that it shows us a useful, though only approximate, matching between a well-defined system and an ill-defined system. The organic chemist manipulates hydrocarbons in testtubes; he manipulates formulae on paper or blackboard, which is rather easier, cheaper, and sometimes faster. The second kind of manipulation enables him to work out *hypotheses*, which can then be tested in the laboratory with the actual substances. Only the results of the latter qualify as *findings*. If a hypothesis and a finding conflict, it is the hypothesis that is modified or discarded. If the chemist's terminology and notation yield too many hypotheses falsified by experiment, they are revised. The fact that the set of all formulae for hydrocarbons of the methane series is a well-defined system is a discrepancy between notational system and reality; but it is a harmless discrepancy that has probably never misled any working chemist.

4. THE STATUS OF LANGUAGES

In most branches of science, as just illustrated for chemistry (§3.9), the practitioner finds little difficulty in distinguishing between his subject-matter and his terminology. The two are too different. Of course, the ink and paper the chemist uses in writing a formula are chemical substances; but that is here beside the point—who is going to confuse a capital letter with an atom? Who is going to confuse the written (or spoken) formulation of Newton's laws of motion with the orbits of planets around the sun?

At the opposite extreme, there is no difficulty of this sort in logic and pure mathematics, but for a very different reason: the problem does not arise. In these fields, the terminology *is* the subject-matter. The mathematician may pass from one formal system to another, but never from pencil-and-paper to laboratory or observatory. (Or so it is often supposed. We shall see in §6.3 that this is not quite the case.)

There are certain fields in which terminology and subject-matter, if distinct, are harder to keep apart. Obviously this is the case with linguistics. All scientists are obliged to communicate, with themselves and with one another, using for this their language, its associated writing system, and any derivative symbolic systems they may have evolved for their special purposes. If linguistics be considered a branch of empirical science, then its subject-matter, language, includes not only the communicative behavior of the man on the street but also, ultimately, that of the scientist—even, in the long run, that of the linguist himself. This begins to look suspiciously like the state of affairs in logic and mathematics. Is linguistics then, after all, an empirical science like chemistry?

Or is it a formal discipline, like logic and mathematics?

With no hesitation whatsoever, I answer that linguistics is an empirical science; that 'conclusions' reached about language on any other basis are worthy of scientific consideration only as hypotheses; and that even the very special communicative-symbolic behavior of logicians and mathematicians can be observed and described from the empirical point of view of science (without in the slightest challenging the worthiness of their activity). This answer is not a matter of taste, but of definition and of fact.

The alternative answer, however, is attractive to some temperaments. As I tried to show at the end of §1.3, it was particularly appealing in the atmosphere of theoretical linguistics in this country at the turn of the half-century, and perhaps most of all to those within Harris's sphere of influence. Apparently it was this second alternative that Chomsky chose.

Having done so, Chomsky was in due time led to refine the Bloomfieldian-Saussurean vague 'rigidity' of a language, viewed synchronically, into the mathematically precise 'well-definition'. Point C10 (§2) asserts that the grammar of a language is a well-defined system. Chomsky nowhere says so explicitly, but I believe this point is absolutely crucial for his whole theory. If it is true, or if one accepts it on faith, then all that Chomsky says is rendered at least plausible. If it is false, then everything falls to pieces.

I cannot accept the proposal on faith, for that is not what a scientist does. But I can entertain it as a hypothesis, and try to see whether its consequences are in accord with experiential and experimental fact. Let us do this.

The reality of well-defined systems can hardly be denied. But the only such systems of which I am sure are the inventions of human intelligence: games such as chess and perhaps baseball; the formal systems of mathematics and logic; perhaps also some legal and some theological systems (we shall not look into the matter). One proposal often made about such systems is that they arise through certain *uses of language*, and of its immediate derivatives such as writing. This proposal can be rejected, but if we reject it then the obvious reality of such well-defined systems ceases to have any bearing on the status of languages, which is what concerns us. So let us accept the proposal of the linguistic origin of mathematics; first, for the next paragraph, merely as a momentary hypothesis; but thereafter, for reasons that will become clear, as a more durable one.

Let us also suppose, for a moment, that only a well-defined system can give rise to a well-defined system. Something like this—a sort of 'Law of Conservation of Well-Definition'—seems to be tacitly assumed in most work on the so-called foundations of mathematics, so that it is not so far-fetched as it may sound. But if there is such a law, then a language (or its grammar), as the source of the well-defined systems of mathematics, must itself be well-defined, as C10 asserts. Then a language, in its turn, must come from a well-defined source, and we have justified C14. Now, the two main known mechanisms responsible for a child's heritage are genes and cultural transmission (tradition). These are not determinate, and hence not well-defined. Therefore the innate grammar-producing system that the infant brings to the task of language acquisition cannot be either of these, or any part or combination of them; hence there must be some additional mechanism, as yet undiscovered. Furthermore, this additional mechanism cannot be physical, since no physical system is well-defined (§3.8). And this nonphysical system, or its antecedents, must be as old as the universe.

A similar ultimate conclusion would be forced on us also if we retained our Law of Conservation but rejected the notion of the linguistic origin of mathematics. The argument in this case would say nothing of language, but would still infer, from the contemporary existence of well-defined systems in mathematics, the eternal (or timeless) existence of some underlying well-defined (and hence nonphysical) system in permanent parallel to the physical universe.

Although this conclusion runs counter to prevalent scientific opinion, and would be difficult to check by ordinary experimental and observational techniques, of course it may be right. But before we entertain it too seriously, we must consider alternative hypotheses. An obvious alternative in the present case is to reject the proposed Law of Conservation of Well-Definition and to suppose, instead, that there are ways in which well-definition can arise from ill-definition, true determinacy from mere stability. Reinstating the notion of the linguistic origin of mathematics, we now have, in Chomsky's framework, three alternatives. We can look for the step from ill-definition to well-definition at any of three points. (1) Physical genes and nonphysical (but ill-defined) tradition perhaps yield a well-defined grammar-producing system in the child, so that C10 and C14 would both hold. Or (2) the grammar-producing system of the child is perhaps itself ill-defined, though it characterizes well-defined grammars, so that only C10 holds. Or (3) languages may themselves be ill-defined, so that well-definition appears *only* through those special uses of language that give rise to things like mathematics.

None of these alternatives leads to the difficult consequences we found to follow from the assumption of a Law of Conservation of Well-Definition. Clearly, we should give the simpler alternatives every possible chance before we agree that the more complicated one has been forced on us.

For language, the three simpler alternatives reduce to two: that languages are well-defined, or that they are ill-defined. Under either of these, as a hypothesis, we have to account for the empirical facts of language. Under the first, there is the additional task of showing how languages can be well-defined in an ill-defined universe. Under the second, that additional task does not arise, but a different one presents itself: that of showing how ill-defined language, used in certain ways, can give rise to the well-defined systems of mathematics and logic.

Chomsky's contribution to linguistics is, in my opinion, that he has made it possible to state these alternatives. The issues are real, and the answer is important; but the answer could not be sought until the problem had been put clearly. Chomsky has chosen the first alternative. I believe that is wrong. I shall argue the case in our last two sections.

5. THE CHOMSKYAN VIEW DISSECTED

Of the nineteen points of §2, only two will survive the present examination. It is clear from §4 that I reject points C10 and C14. C1 is assuredly true (see §6.1). C6 makes lighthearted use of a once unpopular word ('mentalistic'), but is only a definition, not an assertion, so that there is no issue. The remaining points are taken up below, but not in their original order.

5.1. It is very easy to write down the beginning of a series of sentences each of which seems to be perfectly good English:

>   One.
>   One and one.
>   One and one and one.
>   One and one and one and one.
>   . . .

Chomsky's views require us to believe that, if the first few of such a series (not necessarily the particular series displayed) are English, then so is the thousandth, or the billionth, or the nth for any positive integer n. This is empirically absurd. I claim that the millionth—or even the thousandth—term of this series is in fact not English, just as a million is not a possible football score (§3.4). This does not mean that we can specify exactly which term of the series is the longest that *is* good English, any more than we can specify the largest possible football score or write down the formula for the longest possible methane-series hydrocarbon molecule. As one attempts a longer and longer sentence of the kind shown, or of the kind defined by any other open-ended pattern, one encounters certain *flexible constraints*, that are, in my opinion, *part of the language*, just as the time limits of a football game are part of football. Moreover, it seems that *all* constraints in a language are of this more or less rubbery sort, yielding no definite boundary to the 'set of all possible sentences' of the language; and just for these reasons languages are ill-defined.

But if a language is ill-defined, then point C2 becomes untenable. We cannot say that it provides its users with an infinite set of sentences, any more than we can say that the set of possible football scores is either finite or infinite. Just as there may be an informal sense of 'finite' in which the ill-defined set of possible football scores is finite, so, perhaps, there is some casual sense of 'infinite' in which the Chomskyan statement is acceptable. But Chomsky does not mean the term in any such casual sense; if he did, he would merely be saying what many others have said—for instance, Humboldt, whom Chomsky quotes (1965 p. 8, cited above at the beginning of §3), or Bloomfield (e.g., 1933, p. 32). Chomsky's aim is to tighten up such loose talk. But when the assertion becomes tight, it also becomes false.

How, then, if mathematics is derived from language, can mathematicians speak with perfect integrity of well-defined systems, even infinite ones? We shall come to the answer in §6.3, and shall discover that it has nothing to do with the point here under discussion.

5.2. If languages are ill-defined, then the theory of computability and unsolvability ceases to have any relevance for linguistics, since this entire theory applies only to well-defined systems. This knocks the props out from under current mathematical linguistics, at least in the form of algebraic grammar, whose basic assumption is that a language can be viewed as a well-defined subset of the set of all finite strings over a well-defined finite alphabet. Those who are persuaded by my arguments may want to propose that, even if this basic assumption is empirically false, one can achieve a practically useful approximation by making it; compare the comparable discrepancy between molecules and chemical formulae (§3.9). This may be so if one's concern is, say, the programming of computers for the helpful manipulation of language data. But an approximation is always made possible by leaving some things out of account, and I believe the things left out of account in order to achieve an approximation of this particular sort *are just the most important properties of human language*, in that they are the source of its openness (Chomsky's C1; see §6.1).[27]

Current algebraic grammar is potentially dangerous, in that preoccupation with it, however laudable one's purposes, may blind one to alternative formal approaches that would fit the empirical facts better. I have no idea what those alternative formalizations may be, but I am sure we will not invent them unless we acknowledge the need to do so.

5.3.   Point C3 is badly confused. The use of the word 'know' is misleading. The English verb 'know' is ambiguous as between French *savoir* and *connaître*, German *wissen* and *kennen*, Chinese *jr̄dau*, *rènshr*, and *hwèi*. Setting aside the *connaître-kennen-rènshr* part as probably irrelevant, there is still the ambiguity resolved in Chinese as *hwèi* versus *jr̄dau*, resolvable in English by paraphrase as *know how to* versus *have knowledge of*. Philosophical speculation under the rubric 'epistemology' turns largely on the *have knowledge of* sense: it tends to reify processes, or at least to use many abstract nouns and to forget, at awkward moments, that they are abstract. The Chomskyan view follows in that direction, to suggest that language is somehow a problem in epistemology, whereas the very opposite is true.

Chinese is more helpful than English for clearing this up. If a person knows how to speak Swahili, he *hwèi* speak Swahili; if he smokes, he *hwèi* smoke; even of inanimate objects, one can say that a high wind *hwèi* (here perhaps 'is apt to') blow down a tent, or that an electron *hwèi* behave in accordance with the equations of wave mechanics. It would sound very queer in English to say that an electron 'knows' the equations of wave mechanics; we do not suppose that an electron knows anything. But this, the *hwèi*

[27]This is a disavowal of my own work in algebraic grammar (Hockett 1966, except §1 and §4), as well as a disapproval, for linguistic purposes, of the kinds of work surveyed in Chomsky (1963). Algebraic grammar is fun; and it may have useful applications to such things as computer programming. It is only the relevance of all this for natural language that I here deny. The reasons are spelled out more fully in §6.

sense of 'to know', is the only sense in which we can validly say that the user of a language knows the language. Of course, we do say just this all the time; the problem is to be clear as to what we mean when we say it. To make the trivially correct assertion, using 'know' in the *know how to* sense, and then to draw inferences from the assertion as though the *have knowledge of* sense were valid, is a perfect example of Tarzan thinking: one grabs onto a vine (a word) at one tree (meaning) and leaves it only after it has swung to another tree. (Another example, no more foolish: 'I know I was born in 1921 because my mother wrote the date down in the family Bible and the Bible only tells the truth.') In the *have knowledge of* sense, few users of a language know much in any systematic way about their language, though obviously they can quickly discover any number of odd bits of correct information simply through self-observation—unless even their own actual usage is concealed from them, as it often is, by tribal belief. In the same way, the average man has little knowledge of the muscular mechanics of walking (though he *hwèi* walk), and, if he is so unfortunate as to have cancer, is not, merely by virtue of that, an authority on pathology.

All this is old hat, and is exactly why linguists traditionally have chosen to speak of *habits* or *skills* rather than of knowledge. Chomsky inveighs against 'habit' on the grounds that it has no established sense in which it can explain language competence or the acquisition thereof (1964 fn. 3, 1965, p. 57, 1966a p. 43 and passim, 1966b, p. 4 and fn. 9). He iterates the point, but nowhere gives any reasoned argument. Perhaps the point is cogent on the assumption that a language is a well-defined system, but I am not going to try to prove the connection. If there is one, then, contrapositively, the absurdity of this view of 'habit' is evidence for the proposal that a language is *not* well-defined. The term 'habit' is little more than a paraphrase of the *know how to* or *hwèi* sense of 'to know': we do not, true enough, ordinarily speak of the habits of nonliving things (for which the Chinese freely use *hwèi*), but to say that John has the habit of scratching his nose means much the same as to say that he *hwèi* scratch his nose, and is not too different from saying that he knows how to scratch his nose. Whatever difference there is between the first and third of these is all to the good, since 'have the habit of' avoids the dangerous *have knowledge of* connotations of 'to know'. To assert that John scratched his nose on a particular occasion because he has the habit of scratching his nose under such-and-such conditions is not a tautology, as it is to assert that the drug makes one sleep because it has a *virtus dormitiva*. The former statement is a bounded generalization and prediction. We are predicting that, under such-and-such circumstances, John may (though we are not certain that he will) scratch his nose again; but we are also acknowledging that this is no Law of Nature—John's characteristic in this respect has not endured from the beginning of the world and may well be modified in the future. Beyond this, to call something habitual is probably to some extent *explanatory*, much along the lines set forth by Boas in our quotation from him in §3.7.

Of course, merely to say that a language is a system of habits is not to say nearly enough: we must spell out what kinds of habits, and what kind of system. In particular, we must show how an ill-defined system of habits can yield a cornucopial abundance of usable novel utterances (point C1); for there are many such systems, for example the system of gibbon calls, that have no such yield. My point here is only that the 'habit' or 'skill' manner of speaking about language, whatever pitfalls may have to be skirted, is rather less misleading, from the empirical point of view, than the 'knowledge' approach.

5.4. Chomsky is very clear on the resemblance of his competence-performance opposition to the classical langue-parole contrast, and equally insistent on the differences and their importance (1965, p. 4). The differences, which alone might justify the neologisms, stem from his assumption that a language is a well-defined system. If we reject that assumption, we also set aside the neologisms and return, in a general way, to the older view: speech is to language as behavior is to habit or skill, as structure is to pattern, as event is to institution, as history is to sociology, as message is to code.

Point C4 sets forth, in terms of competence and performance, a

notion that in the earlier terms of langue and parole was clearly
an error: the notion that since we 'have' both speech and language,
these are in some way independent 'objects of study'. Even Saussure
was trapped by this one, though with some justification, since he
was creatively discovering the distinctions that must be made and
is hardly to be blamed if he did not discover them all (cf. §1.1).
Bloomfield also makes this mistake, as we have seen, in his theoretical discussion, though hardly ever in his handling of actual language data. Harris noted it, and objected to it, in 1941 (see our
brief quotation in §1.3), but proposed a totally unacceptable
'correction'.

We shall discuss the matter first in traditional terms.

When we observe a specific historic event, be it a speech act or
otherwise, we can talk about it in either of two ways. We can be
specific, or we can try to generalize. Imagine two shipwrecked.
castaways who have just crawled ashore in Fiji and see a car go by,
One says, 'Look at that guy! He was way over on the left side of
the road!' The other responds, 'I'll bet that's the rule of the road
here.' The first assertion may in various ways reflect theories
(or opinions, conventions, prejudices), but is not in itself a theory.
The second assertion *constitutes* a theory, however minuscule.
Both assertions derive from the same event. It is the same way
for speech. There is only one 'object of study': specific acts of
speech, as historic events, in their behavioral settings, observable
in part overtly and in different part introspectively; this includes
certain earlier acts of speech observable only through written
records. Accurate reports of observations ('He was way over on
the left side of the road!') are not theories: their sole importance
for theory is that they enable the theorist to examine the evidence at leisure. The linguist seeks theories, which are genera-
izations from observations, and are about *speech*. They yield
predictions, and are corrected by subsequent observations. The
linguist is led to posit that the observable regularities of actual
speech are a matter of habits, resident in the users of the language—rather than, say, a matter of automatic chemical response
to impinging sunlight. He calls those habits 'language'. This

proposal is part of our theorizing about *speech*. It makes no sense to pretend that there can be a separate and distinct theory of *language*.

What has just been said seems to me to be completely unaffected by Chomsky's revision of 'speech' and 'language' into 'performance' and 'competence'. Empirically, we might be led by our observations of speech to propose that the underlying system, the set of habits we call the language, is well defined. But Chomsky was not led to this conclusion empirically, nor, so far as I know, has anyone else proposed this as an empirical hypothesis. Rather, his opinion that a language is well-defined seems to come first, in a logical if not a chronological sense. This assumption is hardly supported by observation, which, in addition to the discernible regularities of speech in any one community, reveals oddities and vagaries of all sorts. However, the assumption can be retained in the face of the evidence if one posits an obscure sort of 'underlying' system that *by definition* meets the requirements of the assumption, and then explains (or explains away) the vagaries of actual speech as due to the participation of other factors. But this step moves the underlying system completely out of the reach of the methods of empirical science. The notion thereby ceases to be a hypothesis, and becomes merely idle philosophical speculation.

Similar comments apply to Chomsky's 'ideal speaker-listener' (point C5). There is nothing wrong with employing idealizations in a theory, provided they do the job for which they are intended; no one claims that any ideal speaker-listener actually exists, any more than that there are any truly rigid rods or precisely accurate clocks (in relativity). We must remember what an idealization is. It is not what we are analyzing, not part of our subject-matter; rather, it is part of the terminological apparatus with which we analyze and discuss real objects and systems. Now, once we abandon the notion that a language is well-defined, this particular idealization becomes useless, like the now outmoded 'economic man'. If outgrown idealizations were fertilizer, the paths of science would be hedged with roses. In the present case, we can do much better by referring in everyday terms to the *average* or *typical* user of a language—who has, in full measure, all the 'faults' of which Chomsky divests his imaginary ideal. 'I'll bet that's the rule of the road here': this says, among other things, that any old driver in Fiji will usually keep to the left, and that one who fails to do so had better watch out. We need no 'ideal Fijian driver' who *never* forgets the rule (and perhaps *invariably* obeys it).

5.5. Point C7 is typical of the sort of unnatural complexity forced by what I think is Chomsky's basic premise. Linguists have rarely felt that they had to indulge in formal statistics, but in generalizing from observed speech they have at least felt obliged to distinguish between varying degrees of 'productivity' of patterns —in Sapir's phrase, differing 'configurational pressures'. This is important for understanding how people can say new things (point C1). One assumes that, in a situation in which various partly incompatible patterns are all apt, their interplay and the resolution of their incompatibilities can lead to a sentence that has not been said before. The probabilities may change, sometimes rather kaleidoscopically, but for any one speaker at any one moment they are an integral part of his language habits.

Now, by definition, a probabilistic system is not well-defined. Thus, if one accepts the proposal that speech behavior reflects, if only dimly, an internal well-defined system (the speaker's 'competence'), then Chomsky's assertion must be true: a speaker's 'knowledge of probabilities' must be a separate matter, that works along with his 'knowledge of the grammar' and with other things in governing actually produced speech. This forced separation is entirely artificial, and affords us just that much more reason for rejecting Chomsky's key assumption.

5.6. Indeed, Chomsky has developed a notable tendency to 'explain' complexities by positing, ad hoc, more or less independent pieces of mental furniture. As in nineteenth century German 'Geisteswissenschaft', this actually explains nothing at all, but merely forestalls inquiry; though in fairness we must admit that in Chomsky's case the practice may simply be a device for filing various difficult matters for later consideration. We come now to an instance of this in which Chomsky's views prolong an error of the 1940's, though in a new guise: the notion of the separability of grammar and semantics.

For the most part, we encounter no insurmountable difficulty in distinguishing between an act of speech and a nonspeech act, nor in segregating the speech part of some complex action from the nonspeech part. I do not mean that the problem is completely trivial: indeed, we are still not sure of the exact boundary between linguistic and paralinguistic behavior, though we have good guidelines pointing towards the empirical solution. Now, as linguists, we are concerned—perhaps I should say that we are concerned *only*—with those sets or systems of habits that lie behind the speech part. But how much does this allow us to leave out? To what extent are the speech habits, as just defined, segregated in actual fact from the totality of habits that constitutes the particular speaker's idioverse—his whole share of the lifeways of his community?

In the early 1950's a number of us were independently recognizing that the notion of the separability of semantics from the rest of language design, if wrong, was only half wrong. Meaning, we realized, is not a possible criterion in phonological analysis; apparent resorts to meaning in this operation are in fact spurious. I believe this point was first made in print by Chomsky (1955). But he supplied no alternative criterion for phonological analysis, except for a passing reference to Harris's 'pair test', and he failed to note that what is true for phonology is not necessarily true for the rest of the design of a language. On the first, the usability of the pair test implies an assumption that, for the speakers of a language under (relatively) noiseless conditions, some utterances *sound the same* and some *sound different*. This assumption affords us the only possible criterion for phonological analysis (Hockett 1955). All our field techniques, including the pair test and its variants, rest on this assumption and merely adapt the criterion to practical exigencies. On the second, some of us in due time realized (Hockett 1961) that as long as no further criteria for manipulating our data are added, we are simply doing more phonology. In order to get past the phonology of a language to any of the rest of its design, additional criteria must be used, and these inevitably turn out to be semantic.

It is now clear to most of us that, whatever the situation in which speech occurs, and whatever the topic of discourse, what is to be said must travel the 'final common path' of phonological habits. Despite Firth (e.g., 1951), haymaking and lovemaking in a single community, though they may evoke different vocabularies and be marked by different paralinguistic phenomena, do not require separate phonological systems. But, setting phonology aside, to what extent is grammar (or 'the rest of grammar', for those for whom the term habitually includes phonology) separable from semantics?

A certain kind of separability is clear when there is a discrepancy. Here is a familiar example. In out culture a number of cereal grains, all of which are botanically more or less akin, are dealt with in rather similar ways. For the most part, they are also spoken of in similar ways: *wheat, barley, rye, millet, rice, corn* are all mass nouns, pluralized or used with the indefinite article only by virtue of an abbreviative transformation (*an X*, where *X* is a mass noun, is a transform of *a Y of X*, where *Y* is any appropriate term for a quantity or kind: *a wheat* for *a kind of wheat*, *a sugar* for *a serving of sugar* or *a kind of sugar* or the like, *a science* for *a branch of science*). But *oats* is, instead, an isolated plural count noun (like *scissors* or *pants*, with no matching singular). This linguistic difference in no way parallels any difference in the grains themselves or in our habitual ways of handling them. If we had a complete codification of all relevant aspects of our culture, other than the language, we should not be able to predict this discrepancy in the language: the deviation of the word *oats* is a purely linguistic fact and has to be stated separately. This is exactly on the par with the fact that no amount of information about our culture, other than the language, would permit us to infer that the word for wheat is *wheat* rather than something else.

We know that, when such a discrepancy exists, the language habits may be modified to match more closely the rest of the culture or the facts of the physicogeographical environment. I have met native speakers of English for whom *oats*, despite the terminal *-s*, functions grammatically as a singular mass noun, exactly like the names of the other cereal grains. Even more widespread is the treatment of the historically plural form *data* as a singular mass noun: *the data was*, like *the information was, the milk was.*

Rather more rarely, and within sharper constraints, a discrepancy of this sort may lead to a modification of the rest of the culture, perhaps only momentarily and for one speaker, to fit the linguistic habit. Each instance of this is an example of Whorf's impact of language on 'habitual thought and behavior' (1941; Carroll 1956 passim). A perfect example is the case of the man who calmly lit a cigarette in the vicinity of gasoline drums, because he had noticed that they were labelled *empty*. This example also shows how explosively forceful can be the constraints on this method of eliminating discrepancies.

But when a difference in the grammatical behavior of two words parallels a difference in their meanings, or when words that are used in similar ways have similar meanings, I see no reason to assume any separability of grammar and semantics, nor any reason to separate either of these from 'the rest of culture'. In these cases, the 'speech habits' involved are not merely linguistic, but of a kind reflected both in speech and in other modes of behavior. Lees points out that it is routine to say *That poet is popular in Japan* but would be peculiar to say *That poet is tall in Japan* (1960). Of course this is true. But is it a purely *linguistic* truth? Or is it not also a fact about popularity and height in our culture (or, conceivably, in many or all human cultures)?

In a narrow sense—too narrow a sense for practicality— the task of the linguist in the field could be described as that of discovering and setting forth all those facts about a language that cannot be inferred from all the other lifeways of the community. This would mean the phonological habits, the stock of elementary linguistic forms and their meanings (one cannot infer from the rest of the culture that the word for wheat is *wheat*), the ways in which these forms are combined, permuted, or modified and the alterations of meaning achieved by such arrangements and rearrangements, and the brute facts of discrepancies such as that of English *oats*. This divides neatly into unequal parts: on the one hand, the phonological system; on the other, the enormously complex conventions of correspondence between arrangements of phonological material and meanings. This second part is grammar(-and-lexicon) in the classical sense; it is not something different from and in addition to semantics, but, as Bloomfield said in 1914 (see our quote in §1.2), simply *is* the semantic system—*the way the particular language handles the world*. The overlap between this and the task of the general ethnographer working with the same community (but ignoring the language) is clear: even a discrepancy, such as *oats*, cannot be discovered purely from information on the language, but requires also certain information about the rest of the culture.

The reason why this definition of the task of the linguist in the field is too narrow to be practical is also clear. No general ethnographer, ignoring the language, could collect all the nonlinguistic information the linguist needs, and the linguist has to do some of it himself. Especially when a linguist is discussing features in which speech parallels nonspeech behavior, he is simultaneously a linguist and a general ethnographer. It is altogether proper that he should do this. He is not subjecting himself to prosecution by poaching on some other specialist's preserves. Moreover, the special angle of approach of the linguist (from *form* to *meaning*, as Bloomfield said) may uncover subtle but important facts of a culture easily overlooked by the general ethnographer. It could well have been a linguist (in fact, it seems to have been a historian paying attention to clues in language) who pointed to one crucial difference between British and American culture reflected in the fact that in Britain one *stands* for election to political office, whereas in the United States one *runs* for office.

Idiolects within a speech community differ; idioverses within a cultural community differ; and both are constantly changing in details. An individual speaker's information about the things meant by some set of words need not be as complete as that of some other members of his community in order for him to use those words in many routine ways without revealing his ignorance. A schoolboy was assigned the task of writing an essay about a moose hunt. His story read quite well until the last paragraph, where the hunter, having crept through the woods, 'at last caught sight of the moose, perched on the topmost limb of a tall tree'. I believe that in a few minutes' time I could recall forty of fifty common tree names. My ignorance of practical botany would be revealed, however, equally well by a walk through the woods in which I tried to identify the trees that bear these names, or by a written test in which the entire context was verbal. This is a limitation of my idioverse and of my idiolect; there is no reason, in this connection, to distinguish between the two.

The foregoing is a natural bridge to the important fact that in every language people can talk about things that do not exist and may even believe that they do exist, can say things that are not true and may believe that they are true. Many speakers of English know things about trees that I do not. In turn, I know one thing about unicorns that some people—some children, at least—do not: namely, that there are no such animals. There is no sharp boundary between acknowledged fictions and talk that reflects mere misinformation or insufficient information.

So far (in §5.6) I have been attacking, not Chomsky's special views, but the general notion that grammar-and-lexicon are independent of semantics. If the notion is wrong, then it is a source of error in any specific theory that incorporates it. Perhaps that is all that need be said. But there are two respects in which Chomsky's version of the separateness of grammar and semantics is special, and I think these should be mentioned.

(1)   Looking for his guidelines in logic and philosophy, Chomsky has imposed on language a definition of 'meaningfulness' that is entirely out of place. In logic, a proposition is meaningful just if it has an exact truth value—that is, is either true or false, not ambiguous or half true or suggestive or deceitful or anything else of that sort. This works fine when we are talking about a well-defined system: *two plus two is four* is true and hence meaningful; *two plus two is five* is false and hence meaningful; *two plus two is yellow* is meaningless (unless, in a particular context, the word

yellow has been assigned some special and appropriate sense). Even what logicians call an 'undecidable' proposition is meaningful, since we know of such a proposition, by definition, that it is either true or false, though there is no way of determining which of these is the case.

What has all this got to do with ordinary utterances? Practically nothing. Most of what people talk about most of the time is ill-defined, so that most actual utterances are not appropriately to be considered either meaningful or meaningless in the strict logical sense. We need these terms, or others like them, but in much broader senses. In their everyday use of language, people often find it risky to ask whether an utterance is true or not until *after* they find out what it means—and even then the simple either-or question of truth may be out of place. Thus, if I tell you that I have built a simple computer that flashes a red light when a numerical answer is odd, a yellow light when it is even, then you will understand me if I say *two plus two is yellow*, and can pass judgment as to its truth. If a child, at bedtime, says *I'm hungry* (Bloomfield, 1933 p. 142), it is wise to determine whether this means that he wants food, or that he does not want to go to bed, or both of these, or something else, before passing judgment—and a simple true-or-false judgment would be inappropriate. With due allowance for all sort of complex out-of-awareness factors, we have to say that an utterance used on a particular occasion means what its speaker means by it. This leaves us free, as fellow users of the language, to say on some occasions that a speaker has expressed himself badly.

(2) Chomsky assigns grammaticality and meaningfulness to competence, not to performance (C8 and C9), distinguishing both from the 'acceptability' of actual utterances in real contexts. This shields the notion of separability, as well as the overly narrow definition of meaningfulness, from any direct onslaught of empirical facts. For those of us whose principles forbid such escapism, grammaticality and meaningfulness, separable or not, must be sought within actual performance.

The basic assumption has to be that *if something is in fact said in a language, it is allowed by the patterns of that language*—even if we fail to 'understand' it or are unable to 'parse' it. But here caution is needed. There are many ways in which to put a string of words together, and they do not all yield what we should call utterances. I can produce a string of words by some combined use of a dictionary and a table of random numbers; certain parlor games do something similar. The result is no utterance, and all we need know about such a string is that it was produced in this way. A string assembled by consciously violating the common patterns of the language, like Chomsky's (1957) *Colorless green ideas sleep furiously*, read forwards or backwards, is equally unimportant for linguistic purposes: it is fully explained when we understand how Chomsky produced it, and for what purposes.

In our culture, educated people sometimes casually pass adverse judgment on actual utterances with the terms 'ungrammatical' and 'meaningless'. If we understand what someone says but notice something queer about it, like the accidental use of a wrong word, or some features of a substandard dialect, or a hyperurbanism (*people often ask we ministers ...*), we may say that it was meaningful though ungrammatical. If an utterance sounds as though it ought to make sense, but defies our understanding despite contextual clues, we may invert this and call it grammatical but meaningless. In such cases the term 'meaningless' means either that we do not understand or that, for some reason, we choose to pretend that we do not, and the term 'grammatical' reflects, at no great distance, the Miss Fidditch tradition of our schools. This Fidditch sense, except for its knuckle-rapping prescriptivism, has the narrowness of Bloomfield's 'grammar', which, it will be remembered, excluded lexicon. Grammar in this narrow Fidditch sense has to do only with certain extremely widespread patterns, present in almost everything we say: for example, the agreement in number of subject and verb. More subtle patterns, about which Miss Fidditch had learned no rules, were not, for her, part of 'grammar' but a matter of 'usage' or 'meaning' or the like.

The trouble with all this, for us, is not that it makes an impossible distinction, but that it makes too few distinctions. When we examine actual utterances, we find that they can and do differ from one another in a variety of ways: there are many norms, and many directions of deviation from each. Moreover, almost all these norms and directions of deviation require judgment relative to the *specific settings*, of other speech, of action, or both, in which the utterances occur. This hardly needs extensive demonstration; the example of *two plus two is yellow*, discussed above, should suffice.

Turning again from Chomsky's special views to the general issue of the separability of grammar and semantics, I want to underscore that I have nowhere in the foregoing said that meaning and grammar are the same thing. Meanings are things and situations, or kinds of things and situations. Grammar is the systematic correlations between meanings and forms, the patterns by which utterances are built in response to situations, real or imagined, and by virtue of which such utterances are—at least sometimes—understood by the hearer.

5.7. Chomsky's views lead him to insist (C11) on remarking that there are no algorithms for the discovery of the structure of a language, unless such exist in the innate equipment of the infant. The assertion is true but impertinent; there is no reason for the proviso about infants. Algorithms are to be found only within logic and mathematics. Even there they play a very minor role. For example, new mathematics is not invented algorithmically, but presumably by just the same mechanisms responsible for the production of novel utterances in a language (§6). If we turn from logic and mathematics to the world, then there is no reason to separate language from the rest of reality for special treatment. There is no algorithm for the discovery of *any fact about the real world*. There are, at best, *discovery procedures:* more or less systematized and channeled methods of trial-and-error, not guaranteed to be successful, but the best we have and, by virtue of the fundamental nature of the world, the best we can hope to have. In this regard, language is exactly on a par with all other natural phenomena.

This particular view of Chomsky's is apparently tied very closely to his dissatisfaction with the methods of his predecessors of the 1940's. For we hear the same dreary refrain over and over again: in each new piece from his pen it appears at least in a footnote (e.g., Chomsky and Halle 1965, fn. 3). And it is all beside the point, because we 'structural' linguists were not seeking algorithms where they cannot exist. Indeed, when one listens to the oral expositions of transformationalists, as at meetings of the Linguistic Society of America, one observes that, apart from bits of jargon (much like the compulsory ritual salutation to Stalin at the beginning of an otherwise sober scientific article at one stage in the history of Soviet science), the trial-and-error manipulation of data is entirely the same in spirit as it was in the 1940's. How else could it be?

This is not to deny Chomsky's consistency. If the grammar of a language were indeed a well-defined system, then point C11 would follow. Contrapositively, if C11 is nonsense, as I believe, then the premise from which it is derived must be rejected. The grammar of a language, *in Chomsky's sense*, simply does not exist. The search for it, suggested by C16, is a snipe hunt. So, also, is any search for a 'general grammar' or 'grammar-producing system' *as Chomsky defines it* (C12, C13, C17), though it is both possible and desirable to seek cross-language generalizations—*inductively*, as Bloomfield said years ago and as is customary in all other branches of science.

Chomsky proposes that it does not matter what kind of evidence a linguist uses, nor how he manipulates that evidence, as long as he comes up with a correct grammar. I assert, on the contrary, that Chomsky's notion of a 'correct grammar' is vacuous, and that it matters a great deal what methods of observation and collation the linguist uses: there is a sizable heritage of techniques of obser- vation, collation, and statement that the novice should learn by apprenticeship before he strikes out on his own, though if he can then add useful new twists nothing could be more welcome. Heuristics and theoretical frame of reference are not the same thing (as far as I know, no one has ever claimed that they were), but they are both important, and they are closely related, and our pre- Chomskyan fashion of treating theoretical issues in heuristic and 'operational' terms, however unsuccessful or misleading some efforts along this line may have been, was at bottom sound.

The test of a proposed grammar *for* a language—what we used to be able to call simply a 'description of a language'—cannot be how well it agrees with the 'competence of the ideal speaker-listener', which is a second- or third-order fiction, not part of our data but only, if we use the notion at all, part of our terminology for processing those data. (In the same way, it would be quite wrong to assume that nineteenth-century thermodynamicists were talking *about* 'ideal gasses'; an 'ideal gas' was part of their apparatus for dealing with *real* gasses.) The test also cannot be, as some under Chomsky's influence have suggested, agreement with the 'intuition' of real speaker-listeners. We have no access to such intuition save through what an informant tells us about his language, and this is often incorrect or misleading. If an informant's reports about his language are correct, they are correct because they reflect his actual speech habits. This we can judge only by independently ascertaining what those habits are. No; the test of a proposed description of a language can only be what it always has been—how well it accounts for utterances that had not yet been observed when the description was formulated.

On this score, we know that no existing description of any language is totally successful. Perhaps we should like to do better; but we ought to be realistic in our aims. The notion that a description of a language could possibly be 'complete' in any exact sense is a fallacy stemming from the assumption that a language is well-defined. And the constraints of motivation are probably even narrower than those of realism. When Johnny got interested in butterflies, his mother brought home from the public library a thick book on the subject which, according to Johnny's later report, told him much more about butterflies than he wanted to know. A characterization of a language that even vaguely approximated the ill-defined 'completeness' would probably be like the butterfly book—fit, at best, to feed into a computer for some application, or as a reference work in which to look up specific facts when the occasions for wanting to know those specific facts actually arose. But then there would be the difficulty that many of those facts would be out of date by the time they were needed (§5.10).

Apart from such rapidly changing details of a language, it is true that some of the problems we encounter in working on specific languages are so puzzling that, if we could, we would dispatch a plea for help to Number 70 Simmery Axe. Sometimes these puzzling problems are 'solved' by blaming the whole thing on the inadequacies of the users of the language. A whole generation of Western students of Chinese did this when, finding it impossible to account for all the privileges of occurrence of the completive particle *le*, they decided that it was often thrown in 'merely for euphony' (compare the treatment by Chao 1965). Many a continental student of English, similarly, despairs of understanding the difference between the past tense and the present perfect, and is tempted to characterize our selection of the one or the other as a matter of whimsy—which it definitely is not (Joos 1964). Another attested response to difficulties of analysis is to give up work on particular languages as they actually are, and to invent one's own ideal universe instead—a retreat to comfortable armchair speculation. This is how the Chomskyites manage to set aside—presumably only for later consideration, but in view of their announced program one wonders—'an enormous number of utterances which do not in the strict sense represent any sentences at all' (Postal 1964b, p. 232). But there is also an honest course of action in the face of puzzles: to admit defeat, perhaps because one's approach has been faulty or one's analytical tools inadequate, hopefully only temporary but possibly permanent (at least for the particular investigator). The best of our inherited descriptions of languages contain admissions of this sort, and their authors should be honored for their honesty, not pitied for their shortcomings (as Chomsky so often does: e.g., 1965, p. 5).

As to cross-language generalizations: we must remember that theoretical linguistics and work with specific languages stand in a dialectic complementation. Chomsky proposes that 'practice' is dependent on the availability of a correct 'theory', but this has never been the case in the history of science or in the evolution of the human species. Neither of these two leads the other. Our theories of the moment derive from the available facts about various languages; those theories guide our practice as an investigator studies a specific language, but do not prevent him from discovering facts that require a revision of the theory. For generalizations, we are in an incomparably better position today than Bloomfield and his colleagues were in, say, the 1920's and 1930's. Early in his career, Bloomfield ventured various cross-language generalizations (e.g. 1914, 1916). But then, by virtue of his own work with Tagalog and with Algonquian, he came to realize how unreliable were our reports on most of the languages of the world and how terribly inadequate, as a statistical sample, were the few reliable accounts. Honesty forced him to a conservatism on such matters: in his 1933 book he proposed, in effect, a moratorium on overprecise generalizations until adequate data had become available (esp. p. 20). By virtue of the hard work of several hundred dedicated artisans, we can now safely begin to lift the embargo: witness Greenberg (1963). Of course, caution is still required, but that will always be true. Transformations are an important tool in this new and better-based round of searching for language universals, and the transformationalists are actively helping in it. Their stated aims are commendable. But their contributions are despite, not because of, Chomsky's antiscientific bias.

5.8. If we delete the metaphysics from C12 and interpret it in the obvious way, it becomes simply a peculiar formulation of something that we have all known for a long time: that almost any human child can and, if he survives, almost inevitably will learn a language, but that both human genes and the human condition are prerequisites (Brown 1958, pp. 186-93). Chomsky's expression of this is weirdly misleading (1965 pp. 58-9):

It is clear why the view that all knowledge derives solely from the senses by elementary operations of association and "generalization" should have had much appeal in the context of eighteenth-century struggles for scientific naturalism. However, there is surely no reason today for taking seriously a position that attributes a complex human achievement entirely to months (or at most years) of experience, rather than to millions of years of evolution or to principles of neural organization that may be even more deeply grounded in physical law — a position that would, furthermore, yield the conclusion that man is, apparently, unique among animals in the way in which he acquires knowledge. Such a position is particularly implausible with regard to language, an aspect of the child's world that is a human creation and would naturally be expected to reflect intrinsic human capacity in its internal organization.

This is shadow-boxing. Chomsky chooses an irrelevant adversary. The alternative to his 'rationalist' views is not eighteenth-century 'scientific naturalism', but twentieth-century empirical science, built on the findings of hundreds of dedicated investigators. Chomsky has heard of genes, but gives no sign that he knows anything of cultural transmission, which is far more widespread than our own species, and which is just as 'biological' a mechanism as are genes. As far as we know, it is by just such mechanisms that 'millions of years of evolution' can transmit results to any specific organism, human or other.[28]

Of course, the completely isolated child does not learn a language, nor does the chimpanzee infant raised in a human household. We know a good deal about how a language is learned—by a human child. We do not know why, nor in just what way, human genes (and the resulting human physiology and anatomy) are crucial. This is a problem to which psychologists could well devote themselves; but they cannot attempt this unless they are prepared to accept, as points of departure, the established findings of genetics, anthropology, and linguistics. Surely, we should like

[28]Genes and tradition are surely the principal mechanisms for human beings; but there are a few others known or suspected for some species, and for completeness we should itemize these. (1) Maternal effects shape the offspring according to the genetically determined anatomical structure of the dam, so that an individual's structure may be partly determined by his dam's genes rather than his own. (2) A susceptibility to mammary cancer is transmitted among mice from dam to female offspring via the milk suckled by the offspring; there may be other instances of the 'milk factor'. (3) Twenty years ago geneticists were speaking tentatively of 'plasmogenes', things like genes in the body of the cell rather than in the nucleus. I do not know whether this guess has been confirmed. (4) Flatworms have been trained to run a maze, then crushed and fed to untrained flatworms, whereupon the latter acquire some knowledge of the maze. Perhaps this 'inheritance by cannibalism' occurs elsewhere than in the laboratory. (5) One might wish to mention the constant, or slowly and cyclically changing, properties of the physicogeographical environment. No mutation is going to produce an organism not subject to the law of gravity.

further and more detailed information along these lines. Chomsky's orientation does not afford it, and seems, if anything, to point inquiry directly away from any sensible empirical search.

5.9. Point C15 proposes a model for the design of the grammar of a language; that is, for what I would simply call the language. Although we have already found abundant reason to discard the notion that a language has a grammar in Chomsky's sense, we might suspect that, despite C18, this model could be viewed instead as one for the structure of the set of habits that, in our view, constitutes a language.

I know of no evidence suggesting that language habits are organized to resemble this proposed model, any more than they seem to resemble Lamb's stratificational model, except in this one respect: that phonological habits (that is, habits of pronunciation and hearing) are clearly distinct from all others. But this Chomsky in effect denies, because by the 'phonological component' he means what most of us call morphophonemics.

Chomsky's suggestion that the 'semantic component' may be the same for all languages was made only in passing and probably should not be taken too seriously; I shall be brief. I can discern no sensible interpretation of this suggestion, unless it is just a reminder that we are all human and all live (as yet) on the same planet. But specific differences of physicogeographical environment, of genes, and of culture are just as important as the constants for all human communities. Empirically, one cannot be more interested in the communis than in the propriae, nor vice versa, since methodologically neither can be investigated without due attention to the other.

5.10. Point C19 prolongs the first of the three errors inherited, by Chomsky and many of the rest of us, from the 1940's (§1.3). It is particularly unfortunate, in that those who accept it cut themselves off from some of the most noble of the results achieved by our predecessors; thus some of Chomsky's students (especially Postal, forthcoming) are trying to invent historical linguistics all over again, and are repeating the mistakes of the first half of the nineteenth century. It is wasteful for the ontogeny of a 'school' to recapitulate the phylogeny of a discipline. One of my main reasons for having become suspicious of Chomsky's views, before I took the trouble really to study them carefully, was that they appeared to be in conflict with what has been discovered about linguistic change.

This, of course, is not mere ancestor-worship on my part. We all reject alchemy and astrology, despite the fact that hundreds of brilliant scholars devoted their lives to those subjects. At the same time, the fact that Tycho Brahe and Sir Isaac Newton retained astrological beliefs does not prevent us from accepting their real discoveries. Science is cumulative; this does not mean that we accept the findings of predecessors uncritically. My conviction that analogy, borrowing, and sound change are the major mechanisms of linguistic change is not predicated on a blind faith in Brugmann, Leskien, and company. Rather, my respect for them is based on the fact that, by paying honest attention to the evidence, even when it forced them to set their own personal predilections aside, they found that the evidence overwhelmingly supported the hypothesis—as, indeed, it still does. This does not mean that I accept the neogrammarian hypothesis as 'true' in the absolutistic logical sense. It is simply so much more adequate than any alternative yet proposed that there is no contest.[29]

In dealing with a well-defined system, such as chess, it is obligatory to distinguish between true system-changing events (say, the

[29]At the summer meeting of the Linguistic Society of America in Bloomington, 1964, Postal delivered a paper on linguistic change, on which I commented favorably to the effect that he might actually have discovered a theory of phonological change more adequate than the neogrammarian theory. I do not regret the remark, for challenges to inherited doctrine are always in order, provided they are well-founded. However, more deliberate study, made possible by Postal's kindness in transmitting portions of his forthcoming book to me, forces me to the conclusion that his proposals repeat the unworkable guesses of the earlier nineteenth century, merely rephrased within the Chomskyan framework. That framework denies analogy (and largely ignores borrowing); hence the neogrammarian hypothesis is made to look as though it proposed sound change as the *only* mechanism for *all* changes in a language—which is obviously nonsense. The neogrammarian hypothesis, though still growing and changing, was more integrated than that even in the 1880's.

change of a rule by an international congress) and mere fluctuations in style of play within the rules. Even for an ill-defined system like football the distinction is legitimate, for there are indeed explicit rules and these are in fact changed from time to time by the properly constituted authorities. What we know of linguistic change shows that a language is not like this. A language is a kind of system in which *every actual utterance*, whether spoken aloud or merely thought to oneself, at one and the same time by and large *conforms* to (or *manifests*) the system, and changes the system, however slightly. The distinction between system-conforming and system-changing events *cannot, in principle, be made*. It should be noted that this assertion rejects not only Chomsky's point of view, but also certain of the expressed views (if not the actual ones) of Saussure and of Bloomfield (§1.1).

To be sure, most actual utterances alter the speech habits of the speaker, or of his hearers, only very slightly; though, by way of contrast to this, we are occasionally lucky enough to spot a specific utterance or small set of utterances that have played a part in a more noticeable change. To be sure, also, the practical exigencies of communication guarantee that, in general, the language habits of the members of a single community change in parallel ways, though with plenty of elbow room for idiosyncrasies characteristic of subgroups or of individuals. When the aim of our investigation into a language is 'synchronic' or 'descriptive' we choose, quite legitimately, to ignore the innumerable tiny changes that are going on during the period of our investigation, most of which would escape detection anyway, as well as the obvious personal idiosyncrasies. We have to remember that we have done this. If a man take a snapshot of a horserace, he must not be surprised that the horses in the picture are not moving. We get a stable picture of the language because that is what we have sought. Even if our work is very expertly done, we must not promote our more or less standardized by-and-large characterization of the language to the status of a monolithic 'ideal', nor infer that because we can achieve a fixed characterization some such monolithic 'ideal' exists, in the lap of God or in the brain of each individual speaker.

Yet an approximation is valid, for reasons the discussion of which brings us full circle. At the end of §4 we described Chomsky's central fallacy as that of gazing on stability and seeing well-definition. Well-defined a language is not, but it indeed has many stabilities of many orders. Some features are replaced very rapidly; others persist for centuries or millennia. A bit of family humor unintelligible to outsiders (and thus difficult to illustrate realistically) may last for a day or so or perhaps only for a few minutes; yet while it lasts it is part of the family dialect. The ancient Indo-European pattern of singular, dual, and plural survives still today in English, not in noun inflection (as in classical Greek and Sanskrit), but in the distinction maintained in formal discourse between the *better* of two and the *best* of three or more, or between *between* two things and *among* three or more. These varying degrees of stability pretty well delimit the task of the field worker. He will ignore those features (even if detected) that seem so unstable that they are probably due to disappear by the time his account of the language is ready for use. He may guess wrong about some of these, of course, since the future fate of a feature is never a matter of certainty. He may also ignore, or not even notice, some features, because they are *too* stable: not significant for the particular language, because they are recurrent in every language on which he has any information, as though they were simply part of being a language, part of the heritage shared by all existing languages from that remote epoch when language began. We all know, however, how many bad guesses have been made in this regard, in hundreds of totally inadequate accounts of specific languages (e.g., Alphonse 1956); as professionals, we have learned that it is better to err in the direction of mentioning the redundant than in that of excluding the distinctive.

Now suppose, on the other hand, that the aim of the investigation of a particular language is not synchronic but diachronic: we want to find out how it is changing. The data are the same, but we will register them differently. We will seek, and manage to observe some of, the tiny fluctuations of usage most of which leave no lasting imprint. We will find larger fluctuations: various innovations, fashions, and obsolescences. Some changes, however, are individually so tiny and cumulatively so slow to produce measurable results that we cannot see them at all merely by examining the language during, say, one lifetime. Lacking other sorts of evidence, such as records of earlier stages, we might conclude that there is a large core invariant under the obvious surface fluctuations, a core that is not merely stable but well-defined.

But we do have indirect evidence of past speech habits, and are therefore, if we pay attention to the evidence, saved from the erroneous conclusion we were about to reach.

Imagine someone who had never before seen a clock catching sight of the hour hand of a modern electric clock (the kind run by an induction motor) and noticing that it points directly at the three. Later he glances at the clock again and notices that the hand is now pointing at the four. He makes the brilliant inference that the hand has moved, and he formulates two alternative theories about its motion. One possibility is that the hand mostly holds still, but that periodically it suddenly jerks from one position to another. The other is that it is moving all the time, but very slowly. To test these hypotheses, he watches it steadily for an hour or so. He observes no jerks. He finds that at no time can he see the hand *moving*, but that from time to time he can detect that it *has moved*. This discovery does not validate one of his hypotheses and invalidate the other, but it does lead to the following conclusion: either the hand moves steadily and slowly, or else it moves in individual jerks so small that they are indetectable to the naked eye. But—to the naked eye—there is no significant difference between these two possibilities. This is exactly the kind of conclusion we are forced to reach about linguistic change. It is in this way that a language can be, at any one time—for an observer or for its users—a stable system, and yet be constantly changing.

We have asserted that language is not like chess. But we can invent a variant on chess that is much more like language; we shall call it 'sandlot chess'. An explorer discovers an isolated village (called /sanλa·t/ in the native dialect) in which everyone, even the tiniest toddler big enough to push a pawn, spends all the time he can spare from biological and economic necessities playing a game that looks for all the world like chess, or kibitzing as others play. He asks them to tell him the rules of the game, but they are puzzled: 'What do you mean, "rules"? We just *play*.' He rephrases his query and asks them if they will teach him to play. 'Sure: just do what our kids do. They watch, and then after while they try to play, and they catch on.' So he watches. A three-year-old sits down across from his seven-years-old brother, and moves his White pawn to king's fifth. The older brother says 'I won't play with you if you do like that; it isn't fair.' Or he says 'Didn't you move that pawn too far?' So the three-year-old adjusts the pawn to a position his brother will accept. In one game, while neither the opponent nor the onlookers are paying attention, a player sneaks a piece to a more favorable position. Either no one notices and the game is completed, or else there is an argument and the game breaks up. One player moves a pawn out two squares to avoid capture by an opposing pawn, but his opponent captures the pawn just as though it had been moved one square. The first player says 'Hey! Where did you learn that trick!' The second says 'Well, old Joe did it to me yesterday, so I guess I can do it to you today.'

Sandlot chess differs from our chess not merely in that the rules are implicit instead of explicit, but in that, in the formal sense, *there are no rules*—only a changeable consensus. If a hundred years pass during which no one takes a pawn en passant, that feature is extinct because no one alive remembers it (of course, it might be reinvented or reintroduced by borrowing). Anyone can invent a new move if he can persuade his opponent to let him get away with it; when he can, perhaps it is because the opponent will then feel free to use the same move later, to his own advantage. There are certain vague notions of fairness and propriety, 'which on the whole are impressed vigorously upon the child while it is still young'; but not everyone adheres regularly to such principles of play as are overtly discussed; there are contending 'schools of thought' and conflicting 'authorities'; and there is no sharp definition of cheating.

To our way of thinking, sandlot chess is not nearly so desirable a game as is real chess. It is not very much like a language. But it is much more like a language than is real chess.[29a]

[29a]In reading proof, I discover that the prominent Chomskyan term *rule-governed behavior* occurs nowhere in this essay. I shall show here that nothing of importance that can be said using that phrase has been omitted from our discussion merely because the phrase itself has not been used. The issue is not whether or not some segment of behavior is 'governed' by 'rules', since we could always speak in those terms if we wanted to. The issue is whether the 'rules' involved constitute (or establish) a well-defined system, as do those for chess, or an ill-defined system, as do those for table manners or for American football; and it is the distinction between well-defined and ill-defined that one must understand clearly before one has the moral right to take sides in the dispute. If, understanding the distinction, one believes that a human language is governed by well-defined rules, then the rule terminology one uses is not synonymous with any older terminology of linguistics, and one is justified in rejecting the older manner of talking about language in terms of 'habit', 'pattern', 'analogy', and the like. But if one believes, as I do and as I argue in extenso in the text, that the rules for a human language are ill-defined, then the whole rule terminology becomes a bad one: it is merely a misleading, overly cumbersome, and (in some circles) dishonestly prestigious substitute for the simpler traditional terminology.

6. WHAT DO WE KNOW?

In the preceding section we showed: that there is no obvious evidence directly supporting the proposal that a language is a well-defined system; that this proposal entails various consequences which are, in their turn, empirically awkward or absurd; and that the alternative assumption, which takes a language as ill-defined though characterized by various stabilities, leads to no such troublesome consequences and fits much more neatly the vast quantity of data accumulated by linguists during the past century or so.

The arguments of §5 were largely destructive. Here I shall try to be constructive. I shall attempt to show how the assumption that a language is ill-defined meets realistically the crucial challenge of Chomsky's point C1, and helps us to understand how the well-defined systems of mathematics and logic can exist in an ill-defined universe.

To do this we must set aside not only Chomsky's theories, but also much of the rest of the theorizing we have done in the last three decades, returning, with very minor emendations, to our heritage of scientific linguistics as largely channeled to us through Bloomfield. We must set aside all three of the erroneous views of the 1940's listed in §1.3, not just the one that Chomsky rejected. It is, of course, frustrating to realize that we have spent so much time and energy exploring blind alleys, but this is the sort of frustration a scientist must be prepared to accept from time to time. Let us be clear about our debt to Chomsky. We could not now reformulate the classical view of language in terms of ill-definition, had Chomsky not proposed the notion of well-definition and explored its consequences with bulldog tenacity.

The methods of science rarely afford completely satisfying answers, and what is presented below will be no exception. There seem always to remain gaps and weaknesses, demanding further and deeper research by just the same methods: this is how science advances. The alternative, to achieve esthetic satisfaction by ignoring evidence, is clearly a counsel of despair.

6.1. The Openness of Language. 'Most actually used sentences are novel. This is a central fact for which any linguistic theory must provide' (C1). Traditional linguistics has provided for this for almost a century, though with gradually increasing clarity; in the 1940's we temporarily lost track of this part of our heritage.

The essence of the answer begins on page 273 of Bloomfield (1933), in the latter part of the very chapter whose first sections, as we remarked earlier (§1.2), are so turgid. However, I shall not follow his order of presentation, but present a converging one of my own.

We want to know how people can say (and understand) things they have not said nor heard before. The sensible procedure is to examine actual instances of utterances we have reason to believe are novel. Perhaps we can never be absolutely sure that a particular utterance is occurring for the first time when we observe it, but we shall consider some likely candidates.[30]

Jespersen (1922, p. 122) cites a report of a child who, stifled by the heat in a house in the tropics, said

It's three hot in here!

The classical explanation is in terms of *analogy*.[31] We can sketch a frame of reference as follows:

---

[30]The argument here (§6.1 and part of §6.2) parallels that of Hockett (forthcoming-b); even some whole paragraphs are identical. Examples, however, are here cut to a minimum.

[31]Of course, Chomsky rejects analogy, at least as any part of 'competence'. How else does he suppose that he himself is able to produce such strings as *Colorless green ideas sleep furiously* or *Furiously sleep ideas green colorless* (Chomsky 1957, p. 15), or as *The rat the cat the dog chased killed ate the malt* (Chomsky and Miller 1963, p. 186)? Analogy is at work (along, as we shall

I'd like two pieces	:	I'd like three pieces	: :
I'd like two pieces	:	I'd like three pieces	: :
We waited two minutes	:	We waited three minutes	: :
Give me two hot ones	:	Give me three hot ones	: :
. . .	:	. . .	: :
It's too hot in here	:	X.	

All the listed utterances are supposed to be already familiar, as wholes, to the speaker; of course, lacking detailed records, we can only guess as to their actual identity. The dots represent any number of further pairs of familiar utterances. The members of each pair differ in sound only in that the second of the pair has /θrîy/ where the first has /tûw/; in meaning, for the child in question, they differ in that the second of each pair refers to something more or bigger than the first. Solving for X is simple: this, it is supposed, is exactly what the child did when he uttered the novel utterance.

Discussing the acquisition of something that would generally regarded as a luxury, a speaker said:

> We weren't sure we could avord ?—affoid it.

Here the notation specifies some paralinguistic material: the aleph represents a sharp glottal cut-off, and the dash a brief pause. This example illustrates two things.

---

see, with blending and editing) not only when we say or write ordinary things, but also when we try to coin an example of something people 'wouldn't say', or an instance of a form that breaks some common constraint, or even when we set up a descriptively convenient 'theoretical underlying form' to help us handle the facts of some language. A language, as a set of habits, is a fragile thing, subject to minor modification in the slightest breeze of circumstance; this, indeed, is its great source of power. But this is also why the transformationalists (like the rest of us!), using themselves as informants, have such a hard time deciding whether certain candidates for sentencehood are really 'in their dialect' or not; and it is why Bloomfield, in his field work, would never elicit paradigms, for fear he would induce his informant to say something under the artificial conditions of talking with an outsider that he would never have said in his own everyday surroundings. In the last analysis, the linguist cannot avoid inventing language as he analyzes and describes language, any more than the physicist can avoid inventing language as he studies and describes physical systems. Whether any of the patterns that the investigators that the man whose views I am here criticizing trained have invented are viable is not clear; but in the interests of good clean fun I hereby cast my vote for this one.

First: *avord* was a *blend* of the two words *avoid* and *afford*, either of which would have made sense in the context, though with almost directly opposite meanings. It is clear that the speaker was hesitating (probably out of awareness) between these two words. Surely his intention, given the social context, was to say *afford*, but the actual appropriateness of *avoid* interfered, so that, instead of making a cleancut choice between the two, he tried to say both at once. With only a single speaker's share of articulatory equipment this is impossible; the closest achievable approximation is a wordlike form that has some of the ingredients of each of the target words.

Second: the speaker instantly noticed what he had actually said (*avord*), and tried to replace the wrong by a right one. This phenomenon we shall call *editing*, specifically *overt* editing.

In the present instance we notice that the overt editing failed. That is, what was supplied as a replacement for *avord* was not either of the target words, but another blend of the same two. If the phonological ingredients in these two blends are properly reshuffled, we get just the two ordinary words *afford* and *avoid*. That is, the second blend is built of just the ingredients of both words that are omitted in the first. We may therefore call it a *compensating counterblend;* but the mechanisms involved are the ones already mentioned (blending and editing), not an additional one.

It can be made highly plausible that a wide variety of blunders in speech, traditionally classed on a purely phenomenological basis as progressive and regressive assimilations, haplologies, metatheses, and contaminations (Sturtevant 1947), as well as malapropisms, puns, and certain kinds of stuttering, can be reanalyzed in such a way as to be accounted for in terms of blending and editing.

In the context of nineteenth century historical linguistics, where matters such as blending and analogy were first discussed in detail, the concern was with the mechanisms by which a language changes in time. Analogy was proposed, on excellent empirical grounds, as one of the three basic mechanisms, the other two being borrowing and sound change (thus in all the standard works from Paul through Bloomfield). It was recognized however, that there are also some minor phenomena not clearly reducible to any of the major mechanisms or to any combination of them, and yet felt in some obscure way to be more closely akin to analogy than to the other two. Blending was regularly listed as one of these subsidiary phenomena, along with haplology, metathesis, and so on.

Now, the relation of blending to analogy is perfectly straightforward (Hockett 1958, p. 433). In many, perhaps most, speech situations, many different analogies are at work, each with its own degree of 'configurational pressure'. Some of them are incompatible, in the sense that following one precludes accurately following another. If all incompatibilities are suppressed, the result is, at most, an innovative form like the child's *three hot in here*, which is peculiar relative to our adult variety of English but was presumably routine for the child. If two (or perhaps more) incompatible analogies are followed—as best one can, with one tongue and one larynx—then the result is a blend. Hesitating between *sigh* : *sighed* : : *swim* : X and *sing* : *sang* : : *swim* : X, a child or a tired adult may come out with *swammed*, where both analogies are attested.

But this means that there is no longer any mystery about the relation of haplology, metathesis, and the like to analogy. The caution of our nineteenth century predecessors was commendable, but their suspicion that such a relation existed was correct. We may thus list three fundamental mechanisms jointly responsible for a wide variety of instances, perhaps indeed for all instances, of 'blunderful' or otherwise noticeably deviant new utterances: analogy; blending (= unresolved conflict of analogies); and editing.

How about the countless novel utterances that must occur every day, but to which our attention is not drawn because there is nothing unusual about them? For these one may propose two alternative theories. One is that they involve mechanisms entirely different from those we have discovered in our examination of noticeably deviant utterances. The other is that exactly the same mechanisms are involved. It would be unwise to preclude, by fiat, any search for additional mechanisms. But it would be equally foolish simply to assume that the first theory must be correct. The sensible course is to accept the second theory as a hypothesis, and to see whether it leaves a refractory residue pointing towards the existence of further mechanisms. That is what we shall do.

An individual's language, at a given moment, is a set of habits—that is, of analogies. Where different analogies are in conflict, one may appear as a constraint on the working of another. Thus, we do not (normally) say *seed* as the past tense of *see*, on the analogy represented by *key* : *keyed*, because the 'regular' (that is, statistically predominant) pattern here meets a constraint in the form of a special habit. Speech actualizes habits, and changes the habits as it does so. Speech reflects norms of many different sorts; but norms are themselves entirely a matter of analogy (that is, of habit), not some different kind of thing.

If, in a particular speech situation, only one analogy (relative to both sound and meaning) plays any part in determining what is said, then what is said is an exact repetition of something the speaker has heard or said before. The situation I face this morning is the same, as our culture categorizes things, as one yesterday morning in which my satisfactory response was *Good morning!*; analogously, that is my response this time. Now, what has been asserted so far in this paragraph applies equally well to the call systems of our nonhuman hominoid cousins, such as the gibbons, except that apparently a gibbon is forced to treat any conceivable new 'call' situation in terms of just one analogy, which must be one or another of a total repertory of only a dozen or so. For humans, the total repertory is vastly and indefinitely larger. Furthermore, humans are not constrained to following one analogy at a time. If the current situation is partly like various earlier situations, then various analogies may come into play, and the blended result may be an innovation. Indeed, in many such cases what is said may in historical fact *not* be occurring for the first time, and yet it is being newly composed, not merely remembered and repeated.[32]

[32]The more complex a phenomenon is, the harder one struggles to describe it clearly and simply; and then it is all too easy for others to say that one has

Anything that is actually said, unless it is just too long and complicated, may be registered as a unit, and may then recur by mere recitation from memory. This happens so often that we can never be absolutely sure, when we hear something novel to us, whether it is being mimicked or freshly coined. This is an important fact about language, but need not alter in any way our hypothesis that analogy, blending, and editing are the basic mechanisms of the generation of speech.[33]

Any three forms, A, B, and C, that have been registered as units by a speaker, provided there are shared features of sound and meaning between A and B and appropriately different shared features of sound and meaning between A and C, may form the analogical basis for the coinage of a new form X, which is the solution of the proportion $A : B : : C : X$. One can play a game in which one does this with specific forms of the appropriate shapes and meanings; to play such a game is to follow a sort of overriding, second-order analogy. Thus: with his *ears* he *hears;* so with his *eyes* he *hies.* If one can go *far* in a *car*, one can surely go *further* in a *curther.* Of course these examples are silly; an analogy with only this tiny basis has extremely low *configurational pressure*, and it takes some special situation (such as the game-playing we have described) to reinforce the pressure if innovations are actually to occur. Yet even such low pressure is enough, if all other pressures are appropriately balanced. If one has a half dozen underlying pairs, A_1, B_1, A_2, B_2, ..., A_6, B_6 and C shares appropriate material with A_1 through A_6 then the configurational pressure is greater.

---

oversimplified. It must be remembered that immediately preceding speech is one of the factors in the current speech situation. I am not proposing any simple-minded atomistic stimulus-response model.

[33]What is said here about the generation of speech may well apply in general to human behavior; this is explored in Hockett (1960, 1964). It may even apply to animal behavior in general; for instance, to gibbon behavior except, in the case of the call system, for the specific constraints mentioned in the preceding paragraph. For human behavior, similar notions are fascinatingly explored by Miller, Galanter, and Pribram (1960); this is a beautiful, free-wheeling book, and it is too bad that the authors were constrained, in the case of language behavior, by knowing nothing of linguistics other than Chomsky's views.

Doubtless the frequency of occurrence of the underlying forms also plays a part in determining the pressure. The great regular patterns of inflection and syntax of any language, such as the singular and plural of regular nouns in English, rest on such enormously large sets of underlying forms that we lose count.

This raises an important question. Even when we can be sure that a routine sentence we hear is in fact being coined for the occasion, we cannot know exactly what stock of already-familiar forms are supplying the bases for the various analogies, in the head of the speaker; and, whatever they may be, the stock of already-familiar forms in our own heads, on the basis of which we understand the new utterance (if we do), need not be at all the same. Is it possible that the brains of speakers and hearers coin and understand on the basis of 'abstract patterns' of some sort, extracted over the months and years of language-learning and language-use from actual utterances of similar shapes? I do not know how we could test this hypothesis at present, but it does not seem unreasonable. To entertain it is not to propose, I believe, an additional independent mechanism of the generation of speech, but only to suggest that analogy may work indirectly, via abstraction, as well as directly with actual sets of stored whole utterances; also, we should then have the possibility that the abstract patterns might themselves give rise, via analogy and blending, to new abstract patterns.[34]

[34]When I compose music, I am aware of going through exactly the same kind of trial-and error process described, in this section, for the generation of speech, though in terms of larger blocks and often at a slower rate. Moreover, I can begin the composition of a piece not with any thematic material, but in terms of possible developmental structures (cf. Chomsky's 'top-to-bottom' generation, 1957): I can say that it might be interesting to attempt a movement in which the hearer could ambiguously discern either the sonata-allegro form or the form of a theme and variations, or that it would be fun to compose a three-movement sonata in which the second movement (rather than the first) is a sonata-allegro and the third (rather than the second) is slow. With such schemes ready, I can then search for suitable thematic material (like first deciding on NP - VP and then choosing *John* and *ran*).

This is like the proposal in the text that analogy and blending may operate on abstract patterns as well as with specific linguistic forms. But my manipulation of overarching musical patterns is done *using the tools of language:* I have *labels* for forms and for the parts of a form, and I can juggle these on or

Whether or not this is a useful hypothesis about the brains of
speakers, it is clearly a good practical basis for *part* of the linguist's
task of setting forth the detailed facts of a specific language. For the
grammarian, this notion gives rise to the item-and-arrangement
model. We list what appear to be minimal forms, and describe the
patterns by which they are combined into larger forms—without
implying that the brain of a speaker does anything of the sort as
it generates sentences (but also without implying that the speaker's
brain does *not* work in this way). Since these patterns of combination show a semantic as well as a formal aspect, we name them,
and the parts combined, by a sort of metonymy ('the thing that
means for the thing meant'): since, in *Jack caught a red bird*, the
first word denotes that about which something is said, we say that
that first word itself—*not*, be it noted, that which it denotes—
is the 'subject'; and so on.

The item-and-arrangement error of the 1940's was to lose sight
of the source of this hypothesis about the working of language, and
to forget that the basic mechanisms, analogy and blending, can
abbreviate or permute as well as recombine. *Ties* is to *tie* as *shoes*
is to *shoe* as *clothes* (if pronounced /klówz/) is to *clo*; a child once
pointed to my shirt and said 'That's a clo, isn't it?' We have all
heard the case of 'Mama, I want a chee, too'; and we know that
cherry and *pea* are the institutionalized consequences of episodes
of this same sort several centuries ago. These examples remind
us also that the underlying forms for an analogy can work in
either direction: if A is to B as C is to D, in sound and meaning,
then also A is to C as B is to D, and any three of the four, as givens,

---

as though on paper. In just the same way, one can use such tools to lay out an
outline for an essay or a short story. And the grammarian can use the same tools
in building a sentence in a language he is analyzing, because he has assigned
labels to kinds of things in that language.

But are these analogs any evidence for the correctness of the proposal in
the text? I think not. Using the terminology of *theory* and *practice* (social)
versus *thought* and *action* (individual), we may say that these examples illustrate
the interplay between theorizing and practice, while the proposal in the text
has to do with a possible relation between two different degrees of implicitness
on the thinking-action axis. It is safer not to pretend that we know things about
the brain that in fact we do not know.

might yield the fourth as an innovation. The minimal forms of the item-and-arrangement grammarian are only tentatively minimal, and in all honesty he should be suspicious of them (*flip*, *flap*, *flop*, *crinkle*, *twinkle*, *sprinkle* are only the more obviously suspicious type; see Bloomfield 1933, pp. 144-6, Bolinger 1948, Householder 1959). By forgetting that analogy and blending are the basic mechanisms, the item-and-arrangement grammarian is led to ask such questions as how *take* and *took* can contain a 'morpheme'— a minimal form—in common, or how *took* and *baked* can; if one remembers the basic mechanisms, such questions are recognized as absurd the moment they are asked.

Moreover, analogies of the following sorts are clearly functional:

(1)

John shot the tiger	:	The tiger was shot by John ::
The butcher weighed the meat	:	The meat was weighed by the butcher ::
. . .	:	. . . ::
The door caught her skirt	:	X.
(*or:* The meat weighed a pound	:	X.)

(2)

John shot the tiger	:	I watched John shoot the tiger ::
The butcher weighed the meat	:	I watched the butcher weigh the meat ::
. . .	:	. . . ::
The door caught her skirt	:	X.

(3)

She was like a mother to him	:	She mothered him.
He was like a son to her	:	X.

Transformations are analogies. Like others, they may work in either direction. Thus, from a point of view extremely different from Chomsky's his and Harris's insight as to the inadequacy of the item-and-arrangement model is fully vindicated.[35]

The act of speaking aloud is typically a two-stage process. There is an 'inner' stage that I shall call *primary generation;* if we may rely on introspective evidence, we must recognize that it goes on partly in and partly out of awareness. It is 'thinking in words': it is the virtually unbroken inner flow of 'heard' speech, from which we make certain selections to be spoken aloud. On the psychiatrist's couch, one is supposed to read out this inner flow as accurately as one can, with no further editing or suppression. The inner flow is self-generating: it is carried along in trial-and-error fashion in response to changing external circumstances, the heard speech of others, and its own past history; it can be blunderful as well as smooth (thus, I have observed 'slips of the tongue' in my own inner flow, often but not always caught and edited out before they could be mapped into overt speech by tongue and lips). The mechanisms of this inner flow do not seem to be something weirdly different from those observable in overt speech. Rather, they seem to be exactly the same mechanisms, internalized from shared public experience. In *short* perspective, that which goes on internally is causally prior to that which is spoken aloud. But in *long* perspective—that of the individual life-history—public events are causally prior to the private ones.

The editing that goes on in the internal flow is *covert editing.* The norms that play a part in this editing must themselves be, at least in large part, the result of internalization.[36] But they can

---

[35]On the other hand, the paleotransformationalist notion of a phrase-structure 'kernel' must be viewed as, at best, a descriptive convenience.

[36]Perhaps not wholly so. A million or more years of natural selection may have built certain of the norms into the germ plasm. This is also a sort of internalization from shared public experience, for we must surely accept the exogenic interpretation of natural selection; but it is a very different kind. Since any nonpathological human infant is apparently equally able to acquire any human language, such genetically transmitted norms (if any) must be some portion of the design features common to all human languages—about which, of course, our information is as yet highly deficient. The converse does not hold. Some or all language universals, other than the basic ability to acquire a language, may be transmitted culturally.

function differently here just because some of the internal flow is not mapped into overt speech. Everyone has had the experience of thinking of some comment he decides not to say. Norms have not prevented the internal flow from generating the comment, but lead one to keep it to oneself. In certain social circumstances covert editing is especially thorough and rigorous, and overt speech therefore unusually smooth. Much more typically, what is actually said aloud includes various signs of overt editing, as illustrated in one of our examples earlier in this section, and as can be observed in abundance by anyone who keeps his ears open.

6.2. Quotation and Dequotation. The parts of a composite form stand in certain relations to one another. If we ignore everything but phonological shape, then all we can say of a composite form—provided we can recognize it as one, and recognize its constituents—is the order of the constituents, or how they are intertwined if they are. But if we pay attention also to meaning, we get, by the sort of metonymy mentioned in §6.1, a variety of different relations for which the traditional label is *syntactic*. In *black cat* the first word denotes a color, the second an animal, and the collocation denotes an animal of that color: we say that the form *black* (not its meaning) is an attribute, that the form *cat* (not its meaning) is a noun head, and that the syntactic relation (between the forms, not between their meanings) is attribution.

There is one type of syntactic relation about which linguists have said very little, but which is important for trying to understand certain specializations or derivatives of everyday language. One of the very important things that human beings can do in any language is to say utterances in which some of the forms are about other forms in the same utterance (if we could not, there could be no linguistics!). In speech, various paralinguistic signals help to show that this is happening, though with great ambiguity. In writing, we can conveniently use various sorts of quotation marks, not as a direct transcription of the vocal signals, but as a functional equivalent. In what follows I shall use marks whose appearance is a bit unusual, in order that the typography may be utterly clear.

Thus we have such obvious instances as the following:

⌜John⌝ is a proper noun, and ⌜ing⌝ is a suffix.
That boy's name is ⌜John Brown⌝.
Let ⌜x⌝ denote the duration in hours of the whole trip.

In each of these examples the words not enclosed in quotation marks are, in a sense, about words so enclosed. This sort of syntactic relation matches, entirely within utterances (or writing), the kind of relation that normally holds between materials in speech and the things or situations that speech is about: in a general way, the relation is that of a symbol to the thing symbolized. One cannot begin a sentence with a house. If one wants to say something about the house one must use, in the sentence, a symbol that refers to that house. But one can begin a sentence with a word, even when one's intention is to say something about that word rather than about what it refers to. In

John is my father.

the subject is *John*, because that word denotes the person the speaker is talking about. But in

⌜John⌝ is a proper noun.

the subject is not *John*, because that word in this occurrence does not *denote* what the speaker is talking about—rather, it *is* (or, at least, *is an instance of*) what the speaker is talking about.

Language is (or its users are) highly opportunistic. Most of the time, the situation (including earlier speech) has already located chapter and page, so that all new speech need do is to point out the right line. We would therefore hardly expect matters of this 'quotation' sort to be simple or clearcut. Thus, note that it is quite possible to define the phrase *be called* by asserting that (within the confines of some particular discourse) pairs of sentences of the type of the following are to be understood as equivalent:

His son has the name ⌜John⌝.

and

His son is called John.

This transfers the syntactic-semantic role of the quotation marks in the first sentence to one of the constituent forms (*be called*) in the second, or to the syntactic relation between that form and what follows it; and this syntactic relation is then not exactly the same as any of the other common syntactic relations among the constituents of a composite form. This is the sort of complexity we find in-actual usage, in both speech and writing. Indeed, the situation is even more confusing, since we freely say (or write) both of the following, intending them to be for all practical purposes equivalent:

> His son is called John.
> His son is called ⌐John⌐.

and, in the same way, both of the following:

> His name is ⌐John⌐.
> His name is John.

—so that *be called* (for example) might have to be viewed as a pair of homophones with slightly different syntactic privileges. It is worthy of note that such complexities are rarely the source of difficulty in the everyday use of language, only for the linguist who is trying to describe that use or for the logician who is trying to purify it. It does no good to say that one usage, in each such case, is 'right' and the other an error. As users of language, we may recommend certain patterns and frown on others; but as linguists it is our job to try to account for what people really do say and write.

What little understanding of these matters has so far become available is the result of the work of logicians rather than of linguists, but I think that the logicians have not yet recognized the true complexity of the phenomena. Perhaps for their own purposes they do not need to—their aim, as suggested in the preceding paragraph, is not to describe ordinary usage but to distill therefrom an especially transparent and explicit set of patterns for their own technical discourse; thus they are free merely to forego the more outré or ambiguous tropes. However, I believe they have overlooked one phenomenon of ordinary speech, allowing it to slip unrefined into their own technical jargon, where it may share the responsibility for certain apparent paradoxes and anomalies.

So far we have illustrated various kinds of what we shall, for simplicity, call *quotation*. We now turn to what we shall call *dequotation;* in citing examples we shall use marks that curve outwards away from what they enclose, instead of inwards towards it. Our first example is a remark that began as a slip of the tongue and continued almost as a witticism; the format is explained below the example:

> This is how we go to Berkland and Oakeley ⌐?—⌐
>
>   Erkland and Boakeley ⌐?—no,⌐
>
>   Boakland and Erkeley ⌐?—darn it!⌐
>
>   Oakland and Berkeley ⌐!⌐

In this there are both paralinguistic and linguistic signs of editing. If the editing had been entirely covert, the smooth actually spoken form would have been 'This is how we go to Oakland and Berkeley'. The special vertical alignment is designed to show something: when the speaker noticed his first slip (*Berkland and Oakeley*) he offered a replacement only for that slip, not for everything he had said from the beginning of the sentence. The materials in dequotation marks are neither parts of mistakes for which a correction is offered nor parts of such proffered corrections. Rather, they are comments by the speaker on what he has said and on the difficulty he is encountering in straightening things out. Even the intonation and tone of voice of the last line, summarized by the terminal exclamation point, are part of this commentary rather than of what is being commented on; hence the dequotation marks about the exclamation point.

Here is another example: a line from a character in a novel. I change nothing but the punctuation and vertical alignment:

> Do gangsters marry their molls? ⌐Or is it⌐
>
>   frails?

A third example comes from §5.6 of the present paper:

> as linguists, we are concerned ⌐perhaps I should say that⌐
>
>   we are concerned *only* with those sets or systems

In this example it would be better if I could enclose the italicization of *only* in dequotation marks but leave the word itself outside them, but I have found no way to do that.

The affinity of quotation and dequotation is clear: in the former, some of the words outside the marks are about that which the marks enclose; in the latter the form inside the marks is about something outside them. Yet it would not be correct to undequote that which is dequoted and quote that which is unquoted, nor to unquote that which is quoted and dequote that which is undequoted. (Don't try to figure that sentence out—I may have said it wrong, and am about to illustrate anyway.) Thus the following makes no sense:

> ⌐Do gangsters marry their molls?¬ Or is it
> ⌐frails?¬

Nor does the following:

> John ⌐is a proper noun¬.

The point is that the run-of-the-mill material of an utterance, not to be enclosed by our conventions in marks of either sort, forms a base line, from which quotation and dequotation depart in opposite, or almost opposite, directions.

Both quotation and dequotation can be iterated, and one can occur within the other; my examples are perhaps a bit artificial:

⌐⌐John¬ is a proper noun¬ is about ⌐John¬.
Do gangsters marry their molls? ⌐Or is it ⌐Or should I say¬
                    is the better word¬
              frails ⌐?¬
⌐Do gangsters marry their molls? ⌐Or is it¬
              frails?¬   illustrates dequotation.
I don't think gangsters ⌐no, the word is ⌐mobsters¬; I should say¬
              mobsters marry their frails

As with any other pattern in language, if things like this get too complicated neither speaker nor audience can follow, and one wipes out the whole tentative effort (editing!) and starts over again.

Our examples of dequotation have all shown a close tie to editing, and it is perhaps true that dequotation is particularly common in connection with overt editing. But we shall encounter cases in the next section where it appears in a different context.

6.3. The Language Foundations of Mathematics. I shall now try to show how the undisputedly well-defined systems of logic and mathematics can arise (and have arisen) through certain special uses of ill-defined language.[37]

Language enables us to speak of a bunch of things all at once: *The people in that tribe are all crazy.* Language enables us to speak ambiguously of some one thing of such a bunch, without specifying which one we mean: *You can have any of these arrowheads for one beaver skin.* Language enables us to ask for the identity of a particular thing: *Make up your mind: which of my daughters do you want?* I know of no language in which these things cannot be done; the grammatical devices vary, but the essential patterns must be very old. In mathematics they give rise, respectively, to *set* or *class*, to *variable* (including *arbitrary constant*), and to *unknown*.

Language enables us to say things that are not true, and to name things that do not exist: *I saw a herd of unicorns in Sherwood forest.* Perhaps more important, it also enables us to say things that may or may not be true (*My grandmother lives in the village across the lake*—or has she died since I last saw her?) and to name things that may or may not exist: *an albino moose.* Moreover (§5.6) language

[37]Some of the most brilliant men our Western Culture has ever produced have worked on the foundations of mathematics: Cantor, Carnap, Dedekind, Peano, Frege, Poincaré, Brouwer, Hilbert, Russell, Whitehead, Gödel, Wittgenstein, von Neumann, and others. By the 1920's three conflicting schools of thought had emerged (see, by way of introduction, P. Benacerraf and H. Putnam, eds., *Philosophy of Mathematics: Selected Readings*, Englewood Cliffs, New Jersey, 1964). It is not an act of supererogation for a linguist to propose a theory that conflicts, in one way or another, with the teachings of these schools, since success requires information as well as brilliance, and the great philosophers of mathematics have lacked information on one crucial ingredient: language. I wish I could claim the argument in this section (§6.3) as my own; but at bottom it is Bloomfield's (developed in 'Linguistic Aspects of Science', *Philosophy of Science* 2.499-517, 1935; 'Language or Ideas?' *Lg.* 12.89-95, 1936; and *Linguistic Aspects of Science*, in *International Encyclopedia of Unified Science* vol. 1 no. 4, Chicago, 1939), somewhat updated. Bloomfield

makes it possible for people to believe in things or events that are, or may be, fictional, or to be indifferent as to whether they are real or fictional and to talk about them anyway. These patterns, also, must be extremely old.

Language enables us to invent convenient short terms for types of things or situations when we need them; examples are hardly called for. The phonemic (or graphic) shape of the label may be one already in use for something else, yielding a new homonym.

Language enables us to *count*. When the storm is threatening, I can point to the sheep in my flock one by one and utter, in a fixed habitual order, a series of words; after the storm I can do the same again, and if I reach the same word reached before the storm then no sheep have been lost and none have been blown in from some other flock (Bloomfield 1933 p. 29). The words I use for this are called *numerals*. Of course, I can do the same thing by holding up one finger after another, provided there aren't too many sheep; however, it is easier to make up additional words than it is to grow additional fingers.

Surely there was a stage in human evolution when we already had language but had not yet invented counting in words: some

---

did not know that Gödel had already in 1931 made a logical discovery that, in effect, confirms the linguistic view of the nature of mathematics—as we shall see towards the end of this section.

After this monograph was in the publisher's hands, my attention was called to A. D. Aleksandrov, 'A General View of Mathematics' (the lead article, vol 1, pp. 1-64, of A. D. Aleksandrov, A. N. Kolmogorov, and M. A Lavrent'ev, eds., *Mathematics: Its Content, Methods, and Meaning*, 3 vols, Cambridge, Mass., 1963, translated by S. H. Gould and T. Bartha from the Russian original *Matematika: eë Soderzhanie, Metodi, i Znachenie*, Moscow, 1956). Aleksandrov is not equipped by his training to make proper allowance for the role of language, except in very vague terms; otherwise, the treatment is absolutely magnificent. Marxist materialism seems to establish a productive atmosphere in which to work on such problems: it leads one to take for granted an essentially physicalist view of the universe and of Man's place therein, where we Western European and American 'bourgeois' thinkers tend to be constantly nagged by the theoretical possibility that physicalism is wrong, idealism or dualism right. I can understand the current popularity of Chomsky's views in the Soviet Union only on the grounds that its antiphysicalist and antiscientific basis has not yet been recognized.

languages of today supply only a few numerals. (Limited counting of some other sort, such as by holding up fingers, may well be much older.) The invention of counting was at the same time a discovery of something about the world in which we live: that certain natural groupings of things have a property, called their *number*, that may be the same for two such natural groupings just as two sheep may both be female, or both white, or both dead.

Language and writing enable us to count *as high as we wish* (or until we run out of time and patience). In writing, we can do this most simply, though not most efficiently, thus:

$\sqrt{}$, $\sqrt{}\sqrt{}$, $\sqrt{}\sqrt{}\sqrt{}$, $\sqrt{}\sqrt{}\sqrt{}\sqrt{}$, $\sqrt{}\sqrt{}\sqrt{}\sqrt{}\sqrt{}$, ⌐and so on by the same pattern;⌐

or, thanks to the Hindus, we can use more economical marks that are easier to remember and to manipulate because we have thoroughly familiar spoken names for them (even a very large written numeral can be read off digit by digit):

1, 2, 3, 4, 5, 6, 7, 8, 9, 10, ⌐and so on by the familiar pattern⌐.

Obviously, language (and writing) enable us to invent *new syntactical patterns* (§6.1), since the conventions of place notation in the Hindu-Arabic numerals are just such patterns, and they differ from the conventions of any other numerical notation and from the syntax of numerical forms in any spoken language.

This ability to evolve new syntactical patterns also gives rise to various condensed notations for numerals. By virtue of these, we can easily write (or speak) a numeral far larger than any we would have time or patience to reach by counting—indeed, perhaps larger than the number of any natural grouping of things in the universe: for example, $111^{111^{111}}$. To assume that there must be, in the real world, a *number* named by this *numeral* would be like assuming that there must be unicorns or albino meese just because the words for them exist. Mathematicians prefer to think that they are dealing with numbers, rather than merely with numerals, and they resort to various clever dodges to make this plausible. The dodges all reduce, however, to an agreement to talk about certain things without worrying whether they are real or fictional; and this is perfectly valid, since the mathematician's manipulation of 'numbers' like that named by $111^{111^{111}}$ can be just as good mathematics as *I saw a unicorn* is good English.

One device supplied by language for using a convenient shorter form in place of a longer one is the *etcetera symbol*. Johnny comes home from the birthday party and his mother asks him who all was there; he replies:

> Oh, there was Mary Bibble, and Jane Bobble, and
> Bobby Booble, and ⌐?—*you* know!⌐

The phrase in dequotation marks may simply by Johnny's way of indicating that he considers the full roster unimportant. However, the three names actually supplied might under some circumstances be enough that his mother can construct the rest of the guest list with considerable reliability. Perhaps she knows, for example, that if Jane Bobble was there her constant companion Jean Beeble must have been with her, and that if Bobby Booble attended then his arch enemy Benny Bindle probably did not.

In some circumstances there is no virtually no ambiguity, and the dequoted etcetera symbol can be interpreted as meaning something like 'I have given you all the clues you need; I need not continue because you can do it as accurately as I would'. If my wife misses a remark of mine and asks 'Jim's children?' I can reply

> Yes: Katherine and Eleanor and Martha ⌐and so on⌐;

she is as competent as I in naming the remaining five. Under these contextual circumstances, we may say that the etcetera symbol is *precise* instead of *vague*.

When a mathematician writes

> 1, 2, 3, ..., 79

the three dots are an etcetera symbol into which the syntactic force of our dequotation marks have been transferred. The notation, by definition, means the same as

⌐1, 2, 3, ⌐you carry on from here, following the pattern
we both understand for the generation of successive Arabic
numerals, but stopping when you reach⌐ 79.

When, however, he writes

1, 2, 3, ...

the *terminal* etcetera symbol, still carrying the syntactic force of
our dequotation marks, means something rather different:

⌐1, 2, 3, ⌐you may carry on from here, following the
pattern we both understand for the generation of successive Arabic numerals; and you may stop whenever you
get tired; but whenever you do stop you will not have
completed the listing of all the items for which that
pattern provides⌐.

Similarly, if he writes

1, 4, 9, 16, 25, ...

the meaning is

⌐1, 4, 9, 16, 25, ⌐you may carry on from here following
the pattern we both understand for the generation of the
squares of successive numbers as represented by Arabic
numerals; and you may stop when you get tired; but
whenever you do stop you will not have completed the·
listing of all the items for which that pattern provides⌐.

Of course, the reader of what the mathematician has written in
these cases is not going to bother to carry out the instructions in
the etcetera symbol. He doesn't have to—for a reason we shall see
in just a moment.

In every case of a precise etcetera symbol of the sort used by the
mathematician, the symbol in its particular context alludes to a
specific syntactic pattern familiar to the mathematician and to his
intended audience. Moreover, that pattern is always *endocentric:*
any form built by it can underlie a new formation by the same

pattern. Thus, given a single underlying form as point of departure, and the pattern, one can iterate indefinitely.

In everyday speech, endocentric patterns are never iterated very many times, since there are rubbery constraints that sooner or later come into play (§5.1). One of the most important of these, indeed, is the fact that the audience infers the pattern so that further iteration would convey no further information.[38] In mathematics, the actual constraints are safely ignored by a simple and ingenious device that stems from just that particular constraint. One merely establishes the fiction that the constraints do not exist! This fiction works, because one does not actually iterate until the real constraints are encountered. One does not have to. One does not actually follow the instructions in the expanded form of the etcetera symbol; one merely makes sure that one knows how to do so 'in principle' (§3.8). This is the Fundamental Principle of Mathematicizing (Hockett 1966, p. 161), which says: *if you know exactly how to, you don't have to.*

In accordance with this principle, one handles the whole matter by *talking about the syntactic pattern itself.* So handled, an endocentric syntactic pattern becomes exactly what mathematicians call an *algorithm.* Of course it would be physically impossible to write down the squares of all the positive integers. But the mathematician achieves *exactly the same effect,* given the linguistic and graphic conventions we have described, merely by writing down, say,

$$1, 4, 9, 16, 25, ...,$$

where the context makes clear the specific reference of the etcetera symbol. If there is any fear that the notation may not be clear to the reader, he may write something a little more complicated:

$$1, 4, 9, ..., n^2, ...,$$

[38]People do not necessarily stop talking when all information has been transmitted. In some contexts, such as certain kinds of prayers known from South and Central Asia, tautologous iteration is highly prized—and the prayer wheel is a valuable labor-saving device. But in the context of mathematics iteration is avoided except for pedagogy.

which makes an even more explicit reference to the endocentric syntactic pattern, since this notation means

> 1, 4, 9, ⌉carry on, finding the nth term, for any positive integer n, by squaring that positive integer⌐.

Any of the three lines just displayed denotes one and the same *infinite set*. It does not matter whether infinite sets are realities or fictions. The mathematician can talk about them without worrying about this.

The kind of set that can be discussed in terms of a point of departure and a precise terminal etcetera symbol is called *denumerably infinite*. A major portion of mathematics rests on the acceptance of far 'larger' sets ('nondenumerably infinite' ones). Such sets cannot be handled merely with a point of departure and an endocentric syntactic pattern. Instead, one has to establish and accept certain fictions about etcetera symbols themselves.[39] The 'intuitionist' school of the philosophy of mathematics calls into question the legitimacy of this further extension. But from the linguistic point of view the steps are, or can be rendered, perfectly straightforward. This is not a matter that we shall go into here.

Thus we see how language and writing supply mathematics with its foundations. The step from stability to well-definition is taken via a fiction (that of pretending that the constraints on the iteration of an endocentric pattern do not exist), of just the sort that ill-defined language, with its particular flexibility (§6.1), makes possible. *Sanctioned above*.

In this connection it should be underscored that fictions in mathematics have a status very different from their status in science. In science, a fiction may be an 'idealization' of a real system, and therefore a useful part of one's terminological machinery for discussing real systems. Or a fiction (or what may or may not be a fiction) may appear in a *hypothesis* about the real world.

---

[39]Cantor's diagonal proof of the nondenumerability of the reals can easily be rephrased to show the nature of these second-order fictions. The procedure would closely parallel our analysis of Davis's proof of the nondenumerability of effectively calculable functions, given near the end of §6.3.

This is extremely important, since if we were not able to ask such questions as 'Are there any unicorns?' we would not be able to formulate hypotheses in order to test them empirically; hence science would be impossible. But, if one finds out that what one has been talking *about* is fictional, one throws it out. In mathematics the situation is quite different. One is building terminological apparatus for the discussion of all sorts of things and situations, known and unknown, discovered and undiscovered, in the real world or merely elsewhere within mathematics. Most of the time, then, one can simply ignore whether those things and situations are real or fictional. This does *not* mean, as has sometimes been proposed, that mathematics is totally nonempirical. We saw in the early paragraphs of this section how mathematics takes off, through everyday language, from such experiential realities as natural groupings of things, and from such real properties as numbers. Of course, it *does* take off, via a compounding of fictions or of assumptions that may (or may not) be fictitious, to reach extremely ethereal heights. But without its underlying simple tie to experiential reality, mathematics would be, not the powerful tool of science that it is, but an utterly unprincipled game.

In §4 we asserted that the reality of the well-defined systems of logic and mathematics cannot be denied. Are we now claiming that all such well-defined systems are man-made fictions? Yes, we are saying just that. But a little more comment is required; there is no contradiction. When asked by a child whether Oz is real, the dull parent either lies and says yes, or lies and says no. The more imaginative parent tells the truth: 'Not *really* real, but we can *pretend* that it is real.' Obviously, there is a sense of 'real' in which the real and the fictional stand in contrast; but there is another perfectly legitimate sense in which fictions are one kind of reality. There are some other words that have such multiple uses, easily leading to confusion on the part of the person whose parents lied to him about Oz. Mathematicians use the term 'universe', short for 'universe of discourse', in a way that makes it only a homonym of the same word as used by scientists. Mathematicians are constantly using the term 'exist', and rarely interrupt to explain that their sense of the word is special and to be interpreted only within the constraints of the basic fictions that make mathematics possible. So mathematics is a game, but a serious game, not a gamey one. Well-defined systems indeed exist, but their existence is a let's-pretend existence, not a real existence. This is enough. The well-defined systems of mathematics may be unicorns, but they are powerfully muscled.

With all the above in mind, we shall examine Davis's introductory definition of effectively calculable functions (Davis 1958, pp. xvi-xvii) and point out the fatal flaw:

We consider functions of a single variable $f(x)$, defined on the positive integers (that is, for $x = 1$, 2, 3, etc.) and whose values are positive integers. Examples of such functions are x, 2^x, the xth digit in the decimal expansion of π, etc. We shall say that such a function $f(x)$ is *effectively calculable* if there exists a definite algorithm that enables us to compute the functional value corresponding to any given value of x. Let us assume that such an algorithm can be expressed as a set of instructions in the English language. Furthermore, let us imagine all such sets of instructions ordered according to the number of letters they contain: first, those (if any) that consist of a single letter; then those that employ two letters; etc. When there is more than one set of instructions consisting of the same number of letters, they are to be ordered among themselves, alphabetically, like the entries in a dictionary. Thus, there will be a first set of instructions, a second set of instructions, a third, etc. With each positive integer i, there is associated the ith set of instructions in this list, E_i, which tells us how to compute the values of some function. The function associated in this way with E_i we will call $f_i(x)$.

Now, let

$$g(x) = f_x(x) + 1. \tag{2}$$

Then, $g(x)$ is a perfectly good function. Its value for a given integer x is obtained by finding the xth set of instructions E_x, then applying it to the number x as argument, and finally increasing this result by 1. We have:

I. *For no value of i is it the case that $g(x) = f_i(x)$.*

PROOF. Suppose that $g(x) = f_{i_0}(x)$ for some integer i_0. Then, by (2),

$$f_{i_0}(x) = f_x(x) + 1$$

for all values of x. In particular, this equation would have to hold for $x = i_0$, yielding

$$f_{i_0}(i_0) = f_{i_0}(i_0) + 1.$$

But this is a contradiction.

Now, from the manner of choice of the E_i, the functions $f_i(x)$ were to include *all* effectively calculable functions. This yields:

II. $g(x)$ *is not effectively calculable.*

The logic of the foregoing is impeccable, and yet it is a joke. Davis knew this perfectly well: otherwise he would not have written the rest of his book. The best way to see the point of the joke is to play it straight.

The list of sets of instructions E_i for $i = 1, 2, 3, \ldots$, must be infinitely long. For the list, by definition, must include a set of instructions for every effectively calculable function, and it is painfully simple to characterize an infinite set of such functions. Consider the following display, presented in the way customary among mathematicians:

$$1, \quad 2, \quad 3, \ldots$$
$$1, \quad 4, \quad 9, \ldots$$
$$1, \quad 8, 27, \ldots$$
$$1, 16, 81, \ldots$$
$$\ldots$$

The etcetera symbol at the end of the first line alludes (in its context) to an algorithm that may be expressed in functional notation as $F_1(x) = x^1$. That at the end of the second line looks the same, but refers to a different algorithm—one that may be expressed in functional notation as $F_2(x) = x^2$. Before we go further, let us note that the etcetera symbol at the *bottom* of the display, though it looks like all the others, is of a very different sort. To make this clearer, let us rewrite the display using dequotation marks properly:

$$1, \quad 2, \quad 3, \; \urcorner\text{and so on}\ulcorner$$
$$1, \quad 4, \quad 9, \; \urcorner\text{and so on}\ulcorner$$
$$1, \quad 8, 27, \; \urcorner\text{and so on}\ulcorner$$
$$1, 16, 81, \; \urcorner\text{and so on}\ulcorner$$
$$\urcorner\urcorner\text{and so on}\ulcorner\ulcorner.$$

The etcetera symbol at the bottom involves iterated dequotation because the algorithm to which it refers is not one for the generation of numbers as the successive values of a function; rather, it is a second-order algorithm, so to speak, for the generation of (first-order) algorithms. With this in mind, we may rewrite the table once more:

$$1, \quad 2, \quad 3, \; \rbrack \text{the } x\text{th term is } x^1 \lceil$$
$$1, \quad 4, \quad 9, \; \rbrack \text{the } x\text{th term is } x^2 \lceil$$
$$1, \quad 8, 27, \; \rbrack \text{the } x\text{th term is } x^3 \lceil$$
$$1, 16, 81, \; \rbrack \text{the } x\text{th term is } x^4 \lceil$$
$$\rbrack\rbrack \text{the algorithm for the } n\text{th}$$
$$\text{row is } \lceil \text{the } x\text{th term}$$
$$\text{is } x^n \rbrack \lceil \lceil.$$

This does not tell us what three integers to write down in the nth row before we terminate the row with the appropriate first-order algorithm; but actually that does not matter, since the integers given in the first four rows are redundant, the algorithms themselves giving all necessary information. In fact, everything but the second-order algorithm is really redundant. We have told the whole story, in functional notation, if we merely say, for $n = 1$, 2, 3, ... and for $x = 1, 2, 3, \ldots$, that

$$F_n(x) = x^n.$$

However, we have to remember that this succinct notation incorporates all the complex syntactical relations indicated by the quotation and dequotation marks in the last of the three displays above.

Now, referring for convenience to the summarizing functional expression just given, it is clear that for every positive integer value of n, x^n is effectively calculable. Hence for every F_n there must be a set of instructions on Davis's list. Even if there were no *other* effectively calculable functions, that list would have to be infinitely long. The fact that there are indeed other effectively calculable functions means only that the sets of instructions for our F_n must be scattered somehow through the list, separated by sets of instructions for other effectively calculable functions.

But we also know that it is impossible to assemble an infinitely long list. Whenever loose talk conveys the impression that this is required, we know that what is really called for is not a list at all, but a point of departure and an endocentric syntactic pattern—an algorithm. There is, in principle, no reason why one cannot formulate an algorithm whose yield is further algorithms, rather than numerals or something else. In fact, this is just what we did in order to provide for a complete characterization of our effectively calculable functions F_n. And just this must be what Davis is really requiring: a second-order algorithm such that, for $i = 1, 2, 3$, and so on, the ith set of instructions is generated. But Davis's requirements are more stringent than that: he specifies that each set of instructions shall be in (written) English, and that they be ordered in a certain way, a way we shall call 'crescendo alphabetical order' (see our quotation from him above).

Is this possible? Let us keep our faces straight for a moment longer, and try.

First we must determine the alphabet of English. As any printer will confirm, there are far more than 26 characters—what with functional differences of type face, numerals, and so on. Let us say that there is a definite total number of characters, and let us call that number N.

Second, we arrange for a computer, or a flock of stenographers, to start writing out all finite strings over this alphabet of N characters, starting with the N strings of length one, then the N^2 strings of length two, and so on.

We feed the output of this generating device to two screening teams working in tandem. The first screening team is to delete all strings that are not English, and pass the survivors on to the second team. The second team is to delete all strings that are not sets of instructions in Davis's sense, and are to number the rest serially.

This is clearly a *procedure*. It will work in this sense: the output of the second screening team will be a list of sets of instructions, and the operation can in principle be continued indefinitely. But it should be limpidly clear that the procedure is not an *algorithm*. There are difficulties and uncertainties at every step. A string discarded by the second screening team yesterday as not fitting Davis's requirements might become a set of instructions tomorrow by virtue of a newly coined technical term or symbol of just the right graphic shape. A string discarded by the first screening team as not English might become English tomorrow in just the same way. If one fed the output of the generating device, in duplicate, to two sets of teams working independently, they would not agree in their judgments. Some strings will be susceptible of more than one interpretation, perhaps yielding two or more actual (but distinct) algorithms. And there is not even any guarantee that the alphabet settled on initially is complete—a writer may devise a new character tomorrow. Nor, in this connection, would it do any good to operate in terms of spoken English rather than written: a phonemic system is highly stable, to be sure, but rephonemicizations do occur, and if one occurred during the operation then the *whole alphabet* would be changed.

There is only one way to convert Davis's introductory definition and argument into one that is coherent and cogent in premises as well as in logic. This is to replace the resort to English, or to any other natural language, spoken or written, by a resort to a specially devised pseudolanguage that is well-defined to start with. This is exactly what the theory of computability and unsolvability does. Arguments similar to Davis's introductory one then become cogent. However, they thereupon cease to have any relevance for natural languages, because in order to be usable within the theory the special pseudolanguage must be derived from ordinary language by discarding just those properties of ordinary language that are most characteristic and vital (§5.1): mere stability, which incorporates the potentiality of innovation, is by a fiction replaced by well-definition.

But this is not all. By just this same step, the formal systematization of the mathematical logicians also ceases to be of any particular relevance for most of the rest of mathematics. The most startling conclusion that has so far been reached in the theory of computability and unsolvability is doubtless Gödel's famous theorem (1931), on which most of the work done since in this field—even the name 'computability and unsolvability'—has been a sort of calque. This theorem, or its immediate consequences, can be expressed in many ways. For us, in the light of the discussion of §4, the best expression is this: *There is no Law of Conservation of Well-Definition*. It is not possible, as certain philosophers of mathematics used to hope, to find a few initially given elements as points of departure, and a single massive superalgorithm, from which everything in mathematics follows.

Thus, the long-standing notion that the foundations of mathematics are to be found in logic is wrong. Most practicing mathematicians know this perfectly well. One of them recently said to me, 'mathematicians have never let logicians keep them from doing what they want to do'. Instead, the foundations of mathematics—and, indeed, those of logic, which until quite recently was at best only a sort of half-baked mathematics—lie in everyday experience and in everyday language, as we have outlined. Moreover, mathematics develops and grows not by any algorithmic process: the discovery of an algorithm for anything automatically renders the matter trivial, and mathematicians lose interest. Mathematics develops exactly by the mechanisms responsible for the openness of language itself. Some mathematicians know this too; we must not be misled by the fact that when they express this opinion they do not use linguistic terms, because, after all, they are not linguists. I cite three bits of evidence. One is a recent book title: *Mathematics: The Man-Made Universe*.[40] A second is both the titles and content of G. Polya, *Mathematics and Plausible Reasoning*, a two-volume work of which the first volume bears the significant title *Induction and Analogy in Mathematics*, the second the only slightly less indicative title *Patterns of Plausible Inference*.[41] Polya's description, in volume one, of the trial-and-error process by which one attempts to develop a proof of a theorem could apply, unchanged except for a few terms, to the trial-and-error process of

[40]S. K. Stein, *Mathematics: The Man-Made Universe; an Introduction to the Spirit of Mathematics*. San Francisco and London, 1963.

[41]G. Polya, *Mathematics and Plausible Reasoning*. 2 vols: Princeton, N. J., 1954.

trying to compose a poem, produce a sentence, or write a sonata. Finally, and in some ways most satisfying of all, there is A. D. Aleksandrov's article 'A General View of Mathematics',[42] referred to at the beginning of §6.3.

On one more score, then, we find an opinion of Bloomfield's fully vindicated (*Language*, 1933, p. 512): 'The use of numbers is characteristic of speech-activity at its best. Who would want to live in a world of pure mathematics? Mathematics is merely the best that *language* can do'.

[42]See the end of footnote 37 for the reference.

REFERENCES

Alphonse, E. S., 1956. *Guaymi Grammar and Dictionary. Bureau of American Ethnology, Bulletin* 162.

Benacerraf, P., and H. Putnam, eds., 1964. *Philosophy of Mathematics: Selected Readings.* Englewood Cliffs, New Jersey.

Bloch, B., 1948. 'A set of postulates for phonemic analysis.' *Lg.* 24.3-48.

——, 1950. 'Studies in colloquial Japanese IV: Phonemics.' *Lg.* 26.96-125.

Bloomfield, L., 1911. Review of W. D. Sheffield, *Grammar and Thinking: A Study of Working Concepts in Syntax. Philology* 11.619-24.

——, 1914. 'Sentence and word.' *Journal of the American Philological Association* 45.65-75.

——, 1916. 'Subject and predicate.' *Journal of the American Philological Association* 47.13-22.

——, 1917. *Tagalog Texts with Grammatical Analysis. University of Illinois Studies in Language and Literature* 3:2-4.

——, 1922a. Review of E. Sapir, *Language: An Introduction to the Study of Speech. The Classical Weekly* 15.142-3.

——, 1922b. Review of Jespersen 1922. *American Journal of Philology* 43.370-3.

——, 1923. Review of Saussure 1922. *The Modern Language Journal* 8.317-9.

——, 1927a. Review of J. O. H. Jespersen, *The Philosophy of Grammar. Journal of English and Germanic Philology* 26.444-6.

——, 1927b. 'On recent work in general linguistics.' *Modern Philology* 25.211-30.

——, 1933. *Language.* New York.

——, 1935. 'Linguistic aspects of science.' *Philosophy of Science* 2.499-517.

——, 1936. 'Language or ideas?' *Lg.* 12.89-95.

——, 1939. 'Linguistic Aspects of Science.' *International Encyclopedia of Unified Science* 1:4. Chicago.

——, 1943. 'Meaning.' *Monatshefte für Deutschen Unterricht* 35.101-6.

——, 1945. 'On describing inflection.' *Monatshefte für Deutschen Unterricht* 37.8-13.

Boas, F., 1911. 'Introduction.' *Handbook of American Indian Languages* I. *Bureau of American Ethnology, Bulletin* 40, Part 1.

Bolinger, D. L., 1948. 'On defining the morpheme.' *Word* 4.18-23.

Brown, R., 1958. *Words and Things.* Glencoe, Illinois.

Carroll, J. B., ed., 1956. *Language, Thought, and Reality: Selected Writings of Benjamin Lee Whorf.* New York.

Chao, Y. R., 1954. Review of Jakobson, Fant, Halle 1952. *Romance Philology* 8.40-6.

——, 1965. *A Grammar of Spoken Chinese*. Berkeley and Los Angeles.

Chomsky, N., 1955. 'Semantic considerations in grammar.' *The Institute of Languages and Linguistics, Georgetown University, Monograph* 8.141-58.

——, 1957. *Syntactic Structures*. The Hague.

——, 1963. 'Formal properties of grammars.' In Luce, Bush, and Gallanter 1963 2.323-418.

——, 1964. *Current Issues in Linguistic Theory*. The Hague. Also in Fodor and Katz 1964 50-118.

——, 1965. *Aspects of the Theory of Syntax*. Cambridge, Mass.

——, 1966a. 'Linguistic theory.' R. G. Mead, Jr., *Reports of the Working Committees, Northeastern Conference in the Teaching of Foreign Languages* 43-9. Menasha, Wisconsin.

——, 1966b. *Topics in the theory of generative grammar*. In Sebeok 1966 1-60.

Chomsky, N., and M. Halle, 1965. 'Some controversial questions in phonological theory.' *Journal of Linguistics* 1.97-138.

Chomsky, N., M. Halle, and F. Lukoff, 1956. 'Accent and Juncture in English.' *For Roman Jakobson* 65-80.

Chomsky, N., and G. H. Miller, 1963. 'Introduction to the formal analysis of natural languages.' In Luce, Bush, and Galanter 1963 2.269-322.

Davis, M., 1958. *Computability and Unsolvability*. New York.

Dingwall, W. O., 1965. *Transformational Generative Grammar: A Bibliography*. Washington, D. C.

Firth, J. R., 1951. 'General linguistics and descriptive grammar.' *Transactions of the Philological Society* 69-87.

Fodor, J. A., and J. J. Katz, eds., 1964. *The Structure of Language*. Englewood Cliffs, New Jersey.

Fries, C. C., 1954. 'Meaning and linguistic analysis.' *Lg.* 30.57-68.

Fries, C. C., and K. L. Pike, 1949. 'Coexistent phonemic systems.' *Lg.* 25.29-50.

Garvin, P. L., 1953. Review of Jakobson, Fant, and Halle 1952. *Lg.* 29.472-80.

Gleason, H. A., Jr., 1964. 'The organization of language: a stratificational view.' *Georgetown University Institute of Languages and Linguistics, Monograph* 17.75-95.

Godel, R., 1957. *Les sources manuscrites du Cours de Linguistique Générale de Ferdinand de Saussure*. Geneva.

Gödel, K., 1931. 'Über formal unentscheidbare Sätze der Principia Mathematica und verwandter Systeme I.' *Monatshefte für Mathematik und Physik* 38.173-98. Translated by B. Meltzer: *On Formally Undecidable Propositions of Principia Mathematica and Related Systems*. New York, 1962.

Greenberg, J., ed., 1963. *Universals of Language*. Cambridge, Mass.

Hahn, E. A., 1965. 'Franklin Edgerton: personal reminiscences.' *Journal of the American Oriental Society* 85.3-8.

Halle, M., 1962. 'Phonology in a generative grammar.' *Word* 18.54-72.

Hammel, E. A., ed., 1965. 'Formal Semantic Analysis.' *American Anthropologist* 67:5 part 2.

Harris, Z. S., 1941. Review of N. S. Trubetzkoy, *Grundzüge der Phonologie.* *Lg.* 17.345-9.

——, 1942. 'Morpheme alternants in linguistic analysis.' *Lg.* 18.169-80.

——, 1951. *Methods in Structural Linguistics.* Chicago.

——, 1957. 'Cooccurrence and transformation in linguistic structure.' *Lg.* 37.283-340.

Haugen, E., 1949. 'Phoneme or prosodeme?' *Lg.* 25.278-82.

Hill, A. A., 1936. 'Phonetic and phonemic change.' *Lg.* 12.15-22.

Hockett, C. F., 1942. 'A system of descriptive phonology.' *Lg.* 18.3-21.

——, 1947a. 'Peiping phonology.' *Journal of the American Oriental Society* 67.253-67.

——, 1947b. 'Problems of morphemic analysis.' *Lg.* 23.321-43.

——, 1947c. 'Componential analysis of Sierra Popoluca.' *IJAL* 13.258-67.

——, 1948. 'Potawatomi.' *IJAL* 14.1-10, 63-73, 139-49, 213-25.

——, 1949. 'Two fundamental problems in phonemics.' *Studies in Linguistics* 7.29-51.

——, 1952a. 'A new study of fundamentals' [Review of Harris 1951]. *American Speech* 27.117-21.

——, 1952b. Review of *Travaux du Cercle Linguistique de Copenhague* V: *Recherches Structurales* (1949). *IJAL* 18.86-99.

——, 1952c. 'A formal statement of morphemic analysis.' *Studies in Linguistics* 10.27-39.

——, 1954. 'Two models of grammatical description.' *Word* 10.210-34.

——, 1955. *A Manual of Phonology. Indiana University Publications in Anthropology and Linguistics, Memoir* 11.

——, 1958. *A Course in Modern Linguistics.* New York.

——, 1960. 'Ethnolinguistic implications of studies in linguistics and psychiatry.' *Georgetown University Institute of Languages and Linguistics, Monograph* 12.175-93.

——, 1961. 'Linguistic elements and their relations.' *Lg.* 37.29-53.

——, 1964. 'Scheduling.' In F. S. C. Northrop and H. H. Livingston, eds., *Cross-Cultural Understanding: Epistemology in Anthropology,* 125-44. New York.

——, 1965. 'Sound change.' *Lg.* 41.185-204.

——, 1966. *Language, mathematics, and linguistics.* In Sebeok 1966 155-204. Also in *Janua Linguarum,* Series Minor, 60.

——, forthcoming-a. 'Information, entropy, and the epistemology of history.'

——, forthcoming-b. 'Where the tongue slips, there slip I.'

Hoenigswald, H., 1949. Review of R. A. Hall, Jr., *Leave Your Language Alone. The Classical Weekly* 42.248-50.

Hoijer, H., 1955. Review of Pike 1954. *Lg.* 31.485-8.

Householder, F. W., 1959. 'On linguistic primes.' *Word* 15.231-9.

——, 1965. 'On some recent claims in phonological theory.' *Journal of Linguistics* 1.13-34.

——, 1966. [Rejoinder.] *Journal of Linguistics* 2.99-100.

IJAL = *International Journal of American Linguistics.* Bloomington, Indiana.

Jakobson, R., 1929. *Remarques sur l'évolution phonologique du Russe comparée à celle des autres langues slaves. TCLP* 2.

Jakobson, R., and M. Halle., 1956. *Fundamentals of Language*. 's-Gravenhage.
Jakobson, R., C. G. M. Fant, and M. Halle., 1952. *Preliminaries to Speech Analysis*. *M.I.T. Acoustics Laboratory, Report* 13.
Jespersen, J. O. H., 1922. *Language: Its Nature, Development, and Origin*. London and New York.
Joos, M., 1948. *Acoustic Phonetics*. *Language Monograph* 23. Baltimore.
——, 1957a. Review of Jakobson and Halle 1956. *Lg*. 33.408-15.
——, ed., 1957b. *Readings in Linguistics*. Washington, D.C.
——, 1964. *The English Verb: Form and Meaning*. Madison and Milwaukee.
Lakoff, G. P., 1965. 'Stative adjectives and verbs in English.' Paper delivered to the Linguistic Society of America, December, Chicago.
Lamb, S. M., 1964a. 'The sememic approach to general semantics.' In Romney and D'Andrade 1964 57-78.
——, 1964b. 'On alternation, transformation, realization, and stratification.' *Georgetown University Institute of Languages and Linguistics, Monograph* 17.105-22.
——, 1966. 'Prolegomena to a theory of phonology.' *Lg*. 42.536-73.
Lees, R. N., 1960. *The Grammar of English Nominalizations*. *Publications of the Indiana University Research Center in Anthropology, Folklore, and Linguistics* 12 = *IJAL* 26:3 part 2.
Luce, R. D., R. R. Bush, and E. Galanter, 1963. *Handbook of Mathematical Psychology*. 2v. New York and London.
Martinet, A., 1949. 'La double articulation linguistique.' *Travaux du Cercle Linguistique de Copenhague* 5.30-8.
McQuown, N. A., 1957. Review of Pike 1954. *American Anthropologist* 59.189-92.
Menke, F. L., 1963. *The Encyclopedia of Sports*.[3] New York.
Miller, G. H., E. Galanter, and K. H. Pribram, 1960. *Plans and the Structure of Behavior*. New York.
Pike, K. L., 1943. 'Taxemes and immediate constituents.' *Lg*. 19.65-82.
——, 1947. 'Grammatical prerequisites to phonemic analysis.' *Word* 3.155-72.
——, 1952. 'More on grammatical prerequisites.' *Word* 8.106-21.
——, 1954. *Language in Relation to a Unified Theory of the Structure of Human Behavior*. Part 1. Preliminary Edition. Glendale, California [Second, revised edition: The Hague, 1967.]
——, 1966. 'A guide to publications related to tagmemic theory.' In Sebeok 1966 365-94.
Pike, K. L., and E. V. Pike, 1947. 'Immediate constituents of Mazateco syllables.' *IJAL* 13.78-91.
Polya, G., 1954. *Mathematics and Plausible Reasoning: 1. Induction and Analogy in Mathematics; II. Patterns of Plausible Inference*. Princeton, N.J.
Postal, P. M., 1964a. *Constituent Structure: A Study of Contemporary Models of Syntactic Description*. Bloomington, Indiana, and The Hague.
——, 1964b. 'Underlying and superficial linguistic structure.' *Harvard Educational Review* 34.246-66.
——, forthcoming. *Two Studies in the Theory of Phonology*.
Romney, A. K., and R. G. D'Andrade, eds., 1964. 'Transcultural Studies in Cognition.' *American Anthropologist* 66:3 part 2.

Sapir, E., 1931. 'The concept of phonetic law as tested in primitive languages by Leonard Bloomfield.' In Stuart A. Rice, ed., *Methods in Social Science: A Case Book*, 297-306. Chicago.

Saussure, F. de, 1916. *Cours de Linguistique Générale*. Lausanne.

——, 1922. [Second edition of preceding.] Paris.

Sebeok, T. A., ed., 1966. *Current Trends in Linguistics* 3: *Theoretical Foundations*. The Hague.

Stein, S. K., 1963. *Mathematics: The Man-Made Universe; an Introduction to the Spirit of Mathematics*. San Francisco and London.

Sturtevant, E. H., 1947. *An Introduction to Linguistic Science*. New Haven, Conn.

Swadesh, M., 1935. 'The phonemic principle.' *Lg.* 10.117-29.

TCLP = Travaux du Cercle Linguistique de Prague. Vols. 1-8, 1929-39.

Teeter, K., 1964. 'Descriptive linguistics in America: triviality versus irrelevance.' *Word* 20.197-206.

Trager, G. L., 1944. 'The verb morphology of spoken French.' *Lg.* 20.131-41.

——, 1963. 'Linguistics is Linguistics.' *Studies in Linguistics, Occasional Papers* 10.

Twaddell, F. W., 1935. *On Defining the Phoneme. Language Monograph* 16.

Vachek, J., 1964. *A Prague School Reader in Linguistics*. Bloomington, Indiana.

Voegelin, C. F., and Z. S. Harris, 1947. 'The scope of linguistics.' *American Anthropologist* 49.588-600.

Wells, R. S., 1947. 'De Saussure's system of linguistics.' *Word* 3.1-31.

Whorf, B. L., c1936. 'A linguistic consideration of thinking in primitive communities.' First published in Carroll 1956 65-86.

——, 1941. 'The relation of habitual thought and behavior to language.' In L. Spier, ed., *Language, Culture, and Personality: Essays in Memory of Edward Sapir*, 75-93. Menasha, Wisconsin.